The Blair Decade

Month by month – the key events and
soundbites that defined New Labour

Ian Hernon

POLITICO'S

First published in Great Britain 2007 by
Politico's Publishing, an imprint of
Methuen & Co. Ltd
11–12 Buckingham Gate
London
SW1E 6LB

1

Copyright © Ian Hernon 2007

A CIP catalogue record for this book is available from the British Library.

ISBN 978-1-84275-209-8

Typeset in Gill Sans by SX Composing DTP, Rayleigh, Essex
Printed and bound in Great Britain by CPD Wales

Contents

Preface

This is a cuttings job on the Blair administration – but they are my own cuttings. For longer than the decade covered in this book I have kept a diary of the major events, the best quotes, the offbeat and the profound, the tragic and the funny, of an astonishing period of British political history. It amounts to a broadly contemporaneous chronicle which, I hope, is a useful reminder of not just what happened, but why and in which order. I have striven to be even-handed and any personal comment is restricted to the selection of items and their juxtaposition within each month covered.

I would like to thank all fellow members of the Parliamentary Press Gallery and Lobby, a much-maligned body of professionals, in particular Jon Smith (Press Association), Bill Jacobs (regional evenings), Ian Craig (*Manchester Evening News*), Nick Assinder (BBC News online), Joe Murphy (*Evening Standard*) and Simon Walters (*Mail on Sunday*).

I would also like to thank Jonathan Wadman and Alan Gordon Walker of Politico's. And, of course, my family.

The path to power

'Labour's coming home . . . the glory days of Britain are not over but the Tory days are.' – Tony Blair, Labour Party conference, October 1996.

Anthony Charles Lynton Blair was born in Edinburgh on 6 May 1953, the son of Leo and Hazel Blair. As a child he lived in Australia for three years while his father was a lecturer in law at the University of Adelaide. The family returned to Britain when Leo took a post at Durham University. Tony was educated at Durham Cathedral Chorister School and, as a boarder, at the exclusive Fettes College, Edinburgh, where he met Charles Falconer, whom he was later to appoint Lord Chancellor.

'All the teachers I spoke to said he was a complete pain in the backside, and they were very glad to see the back of him.' – John Rentoul, biographer, 1995.

After spending a year in London trying to be a rock music promoter, Blair went to study law at St John's College, Oxford. There, while the country was in political turmoil during and after the premiership of Edward Heath, he concentrated on singing with the student band Ugly Rumours and still dreamed of becoming a rock impresario.

Following graduation with a second-class degree he worked briefly in Paris as a barman and insurance clerk. In 1975 he joined the Labour Party before being called the following year to the Bar in Lincoln's Inn, in chambers founded by Derry Irvine, whom Blair was also to make Lord Chancellor in the years to come. There he met his future wife, Cherie, daughter of TV and film actor Tony Booth. They wed in 1980 and were to have three children – Euan, Nicky and Kathryn – before No. 10 beckoned. Both Blairs specialised in industrial relations law.

At first most friends bet that Cherie would be the politician and the couple did agree that whoever was first selected to a safe Labour seat would go to Westminster and the other would concentrate on making money through the law. Cherie, seen as far more left wing, missed out on selection in 1981 but Tony contacted Labour MP Tom Pendry, using his father-in-law as an intermediary, for help. Pendry advised him to try a no-hope seat, true-blue Beaconsfield, to win his spurs. Tony came third in the May 1982 by-election, securing just 10 per cent of the vote and losing his deposit but impressing Labour leader Michael Foot. Tony then went for the newly created seat of Sedgefield in Durham's mining country, close to where he had grown up. He faced a tough selection battle, up against several sitting MPs who had lost out in boundary changes. After a meeting with local party stalwart John Burton, later to become his agent and trusted confidant, he scraped onto the shortlist and beat incumbent Les Huckfield. At that time he endorsed left-wing policies, including withdrawal from the EEC, and was a member of the Campaign for Nuclear Disarmament. He was joined on the election campaign trail by Pat Phoenix, the *Coronation Street* actress and girlfriend of Tony Booth. Blair bucked a second Tory landslide and in June 1983 he was elected MP for Sedgefield with a majority of 8,281, a margin he upped to 13,058 at the subsequent 1987 contest.

'I am a socialist not through reading a textbook that has caught my intellectual fancy, not through unthinking tradition, but because I believe that, at its best, socialism corresponds most closely to an existence that is both rational and moral. It stands for co-operation, not confrontation; for fellowship, not fear. It stands for equality.' – Tony Blair, maiden speech, July 1983.

'City whizz-kids with salaries only fractionally less than their greed now seem not only morally dubious, but incompetent.' – Blair on the collapse in share prices, October 1987.

Blair teamed up with the more experienced and seemingly more committed Gordon Brown and during the marathon miners' strike took his first step up the ladder towards the front bench as assistant Treasury spokesman, followed by the number two job shadowing Trade and Industry in 1987. This was when Labour leader Neil Kinnock was rebranding his party after Margaret Thatcher's third successive election victory. Blair embraced the 'red rose' ethos and his rise up the party ranks accelerated. He was an enthusiastic convert to what later became New Labour, aiming to ditch the left-wing and trade unionist tenets of the past to appeal to Middle England and make the party electable after a decade of divisions exploited by Tony Benn and others. He was successively the main spokesman on energy and employment. In the latter post he decided that backing a European Social Charter meant abandoning support for the traditional closed shop. Blair was elected to the shadow Cabinet for the first time in October 1988, having impressed the right people with his youthful zeal and upfront style of public speaking while alienating the left over his stance on the closed shop. The party's director of communications, Peter Mandelson, saw him as young and telegenic and Blair's public profile rose accordingly. Election to the party's ruling National Executive came in September 1992 following Kinnock's surprise defeat by Thatcher's successor, John Major. The new Labour leader, John Smith, promoted Blair to shadow Home Secretary, where he famously promised to be 'tough on crime and tough on the causes of crime', a line which Gordon Brown later claimed to have originated. And he accepted that 'Sixties liberalism' was in part to blame for rising crime, the break-up of families and social alienation.

The relationship between Blair and Brown, two highly ambitious men, had by then become strained. When Smith died suddenly – followed by an unexpected wave of public grief – they sat down in the Granita restaurant in Islington, since closed, to sort out their respective game plans. The Brown camp later claimed that it was agreed that Blair would stand as leader and run the general election campaign, become PM and then stand aside for the older man after an agreed period of time, a claim vehemently denied by the Blair camp. Later a note appeared to confirm an agreement on the basis that Brown would stand aside in the short term provided that Blair would pursue a 'fair' socialist agenda. Whatever the truth of the matter – and it is likely to have been a confusion of deliberately ambiguous terms – Brown did not stand against him and Blair easily saw off challenges from John Prescott and Margaret Beckett. He was 'crowned' leader in July 1994. At forty-one he was the youngest-ever person to hold that post.

'Power without principle is barren, but principle without power is futile. This is a party of government and I will lead it as a party of government.' – Tony Blair, 1994.

As Major's government slowly drowned in financial crises, sleaze and incompetence, Blair set out to 'modernise' the Labour Party. His aim was to take it away from the traditional left-wing and union-dominated militancy which, he believed, had allowed Thatcher to seize power and hold it for so long. Piece by piece he dismantled trade union control over party conferences and funding; with Brown he courted the City, media barons and big business; and – most controversially for traditionalists – he scrapped the historic Clause 4 commitment to 'the common ownership of the means of production and exchange'.

He gave free rein to the black art of spin as practised by Mandelson and Alastair Campbell and took note of the glitzy campaigning of successful candidates across the Atlantic, forging an alliance with his soulmate Bill Clinton. His platform reflected his own priorities as a family man with a successful wife and three bright children, summed up in his catchphrase 'education, education, education'. He was an instinctive big spender on schools and the NHS, broadly liberal on social divisions, cautious on the economy, and conservative on law and order issues and family values. He promised to promote a market economy, eliminate unemployment and poverty (and with them welfare benefits), look sympathetically towards Europe and deliver major constitutional reform of the House of Lords plus devolution for Scotland, Wales and Northern Ireland. Above all, in his mind at least, he envisaged a sense of community in which all sections of society would have both a role and responsibilities.

It was not just the left, party traditionalists and trade unionists who detected, however Blair dressed it up, a lurch to the right. In October 1995, John Redwood, former Welsh Secretary and past and future Conservative leadership contender, said: 'Tony Blair's speech [at that year's Labour Party conference] did seem strangely familiar. He has become the thieving magpie of British politics. Every idea that glistens he transfers to his own nest.'

At the same time Blair cultivated his family-man image. Insiders saw it as genuine, cynics as opportunistic, but the public saw a committed and devoted husband and father who would make 10 Downing Street a real home.

'When Blair is not working he is busy playing with his children and keeping up with their school and leisure activities. Swimming after church on Sunday mornings is a regular event. His own leisure time is spent reading mainly literary classics and biographies and watching thrillers, playing tennis and playing his guitar.' – Peter Mandelson and Roger Liddle, *The Blair Revolution*, 1996.

Across the political and social spectrum the view of Blair as he prepared to challenge Major was predictably mixed:
- 'He's good. If Labour has a [football] team, he should be in it.' – Kevin Keegan, 1997.
- 'My former colleagues know that their sole stock in trade as

communicators is their sustained credibility. I fear Mr Blair's long-term ambitions are being served by a crude, short-term approach to media relations. He will live to regret it.' – Sir Bernard Ingham, Margaret Thatcher's former press supremo, 1997.

- 'I wish Blair well. He passes the entrance tests of belief required in an ethical socialist. He puts high value on liberty, equality and community and he seeks to optimise as distinct from maximise their place in our lives. Neither Blair nor support for him will last forever, but a British resurgence of political idealism driving an expert political programme of renewal and civility is long overdue.' – A. H. Halsey, professor of sociology, Oxford University, 1996.
- 'I think Tony Blair is almost too good not to be true.' – Paddington creator Michael Bond, 1997.

By 1996 John Major was looking exhausted, as was his battered administration, split between pro-Europeans, Euro-sceptics and Little Englanders. The PM complained he had had a 'bellyful' of Euro-rebels in his own ranks. Lady Thatcher continued to snipe from the sidelines. The BSE and CJD crises were threatening to engulf the nation. The IRA ceasefire was breached by the Canary Wharf bomb and later by the bombing of Manchester's Arndale shopping centre. Unemployment was on the way down but Major's reputation had not recovered from the Black Wednesday exchange rate fiasco. His MPs were bickering, plotting against each other and planning for the post-Major era. There was little escape from humiliation, even by going abroad – in Seoul his South Korean host had to be stopped serving him boiled dog.

'He used to drink a lot . . . I know how he feels sometimes.' – John Major on Pitt the Younger, July 1996.

'At least you knew where you were with Margaret Thatcher.' – Tony Blair, January 1996.

For Labour a row over frontbencher Harriet Harman's decision to send her children to selective schools proved embarrassing to Blair, who could hardly complain given his own background. And Blair was given advance notice that his own benches could once again prove unruly. Shadow Transport Secretary Clare Short, for example, warned him that his advisors and spin doctors – the 'people who live in the dark' – could lose Labour the upcoming general election. Labour MP Austin Mitchell condemned Blair's 'dictatorial' style, comparing him with North Korea's Kim II Sung. Blair dubbed his critics the 'flotsam and jetsam of politics'. However, Labour under Blair was winning by-elections again. Such local successes, plus the withdrawal of the whip from Tory Euro-rebels, almost wiped out Major's overall majority.

'If you were John Major with a majority of one, would you really want to take this warring, unpleasant, back-stabbing, back-biting crew through another six months of dark winter in the House of Commons?' – Paddy Ashdown, Liberal Democrat leader, June 1996.

Major had no option but to hang on, even though he knew his time was running out. Early in his premiership he had been a player in the First Gulf War, which ejected Iraqi dictator Saddam Hussein's forces from their occupation of Kuwait. Now he could only watch from the sidelines as the United States launched missile raids on Iraq and extended the southern no-fly zone to within 20 miles of Baghdad because of Saddam's failure to show UN inspectors that he was destroying his weapons of mass destruction.

On the domestic front legislation to ban handguns following the Dunblane school massacre proved troublesome, as did anti-devolution campaigns, the issue of gays in the armed forces, the early release of prisoners and school discipline. Education Secretary Gillian Shephard was verbally slapped down by the PM when she suggested the return of the cane. Labour MP Jane Kennedy said: 'For the first time in his life he has shown the smack of firm leadership.'

But sleaze and Europe continued to give Major his biggest nightmares. Lobbyist Ian Greer paid disgraced former minister Neil Hamilton cash for favours and made campaign donations to many others. It was a taste of bigger scandals to come. Then in November 1996 several Tory MPs threatened to destroy Major's majority over European Commission plans to ditch the pound for the euro, no matter what Parliament decided.

'The government has pressed the self-destruct button.' – Conservative right-winger Sir George Gardiner.

Major ordered the toning down of Tory election posters showing Blair with red 'demon eyes', a campaign masterminded by PR guru Maurice Saatchi, who was then rewarded with a life peerage. The poster eyes belonged to actor Scott Woods, a Labour supporter.

The Spice Girls officially backed the Tories. Geri Halliwell of the group said that Margaret Thatcher was the original Spice Girl. But the future Victoria Beckham spoilt the effect by calling Major a 'boring pillock'.

'For more than a year the government has been drifting aimlessly without direction or purpose. That drift is doing real damage to Britain. Decisions vital to secure the country's future are not being taken.' – Tony Blair, Christmas 1996.

By now Blair could taste power.

1997

Tony Blair romped to a landslide election victory after John Major's government was swamped by sleaze and incompetence. New Labour enjoyed a ninety-day honeymoon period before themselves being hit by sleaze, which tarnished Blair's crown.

January

John Major's New Year resolution was 'to stay cool, calm and elected'. He promised to put family values at the heart of the Tory general election campaign. Tory MP Jerry Hayes was accused of having an affair with a teenage boy, Paul Stone.

Labour deputy leader John Prescott was fined £40 for speeding at 80mph, his fourth conviction in eight years.

Tony Blair said he had 'zero tolerance' of petty street crime and revealed he never gave cash to beggars. Home Office minister David Maclean said that most beggars were Scottish and were not really destitute.

Princess Diana was slated by Tories as a 'loose cannon' after calling for a worldwide ban on landmines during a visit to Angola.

Tory MP Iain Mills died, technically making Major head of a minority government.

Shadow Chancellor Gordon Brown promised no change in basic and top rates of income tax in the first five years of a Labour administration, while the current Tory public spending ceiling would remain for two years. Blair promised business chiefs that the bulk of Tory trade union legislation would stay.

Self-confessed womaniser Alan Clark won the Kensington & Chelsea Tory selection battle, promising to 'behave in a manner that is suitable and proper'.

The Tories miscounted a tied vote on an education Bill amendment, inflicting an own-goal defeat.

February
Cabinet minister David Mellor said of the Germans: 'They irritate us by being fat and successful and full of themselves.' Another own goal.

Lord Bicester, having spent most of the last thirty-two years in mental institutions, said: 'I am looking forward to sitting in the House of Lords and seeing a few old friends . . . I shall probably sit with the Conservatives.'

Stephen Dorrell was stripped of his election job co-ordinating constitutional policies after telling the *Scotsman* that a future Tory administration would scrap any Scottish Parliament set up by Labour. That contradicted Scottish Secretary Michael Forsyth's line – endorsed by Major – that such a Parliament would be 'an omelette which could not be unscrambled'.

Major wished a grumpy Dennis Skinner a happy sixty-fifth birthday.

Andrew Lloyd-Webber promised to leave Britain if Labour won the next election. Labour strategists cheered the news.

Major's government survived a censure motion against Agriculture Minister Douglas Hogg with a majority of thirteen.

A bid by rebel peers to amend the Bill outlawing handguns was backed by 115 mainly Tory MPs, but the Bill remained intact after most Labour MPs voted with most Conservatives.

Labour's Ben Chapman won the Wirral South by-election with a 17 per cent swing, turning an 8,000 Tory majority into a Labour margin of almost the same amount.

March
Health Secretary Stephen Dorrell reopened Tory wounds on Europe by saying that Britain would not join a single currency.

Tory MP David Evans told schoolchildren that Heritage Secretary Virginia Bottomley was 'dead from the head upwards'.

A Health and Safety Executive abattoir report warning of the risk of *E. coli* had been shelved for twelve months, it was revealed. During that time twenty people died in an epidemic in Scotland.

Deselected Tory Sir George Gardiner defected to the Referendum Party, pushing the government deeper into minority.

Dorrell announced a plan to sell insurance cover to pensioners to encourage them to prepare for long-term care rather than rely on the state. Council-run old people's homes would be sold off under the shake-up.

Edwina Currie said that if the Tories were to lose the election, Major should not 'hang around' as leader.

Major called an election for 1 May, ensuring a six-week campaign. He made his first speech from his soap-box in Luton, breaking a local by-law. He was then pictured standing next to a wheelless McLaren racing car, which quickly became a metaphor for his party. The *Sun* dumped Major and backed Blair.

Major refused to publish Sir Gordon Downey's report on the cash-for-questions scandal until after the general election. Leaks suggested that a former Northern Ireland minister and other Tory MPs had taken bribes of up to £25,000 to table parliamentary questions on behalf of Harrods owner Mohammed al-Fayed. Major described the allegations as 'junk'.

Former Scottish Office minister Allan Stewart was hit by claims of a close relationship with Catherine 'Bunny' Knight, a married woman he met at a drying-out clinic. He quit his Eastwood seat, suffered a mental breakdown and was hospitalised under the Mental Health Act.

1997

Tim Smith, victor at Beaconsfield against Tony Blair, resigned over cash-for-questions. Former trade minister Neil Hamilton didn't. Hamilton's wife Christine said of reporters doorstepping a Sunday service in his constituency of Tatton: 'Get those greasy reptiles off the church daffodils.' Labour and the Liberal Democrats agreed to field a joint anti-sleaze candidate against him.

Piers Merchant, parliamentary aide to Cabinet minister Peter Lilley, was caught canoodling in a park with 17-year-old club hostess Anna Cox. He refused to resign. Scottish Tory chairman Sir Michael Hirst did resign, though, over an alleged gay affair, which he admitted, 'may, I fear, cause embarrassment to the party in the current climate'.

Sir Alan Walters, Margaret Thatcher's economic guru, said of Major: 'He lacks moral courage, vision and leadership. He is a weakling.'

'You can put on a miniskirt but it won't make you a Spice Girl. You can put on suede shoes but it won't make you a successful Chancellor.' – Kenneth Clarke on Gordon Brown.

April
Major tried to sideline sleaze as an election issue, saying: 'If there's an anti-sleaze candidate, it's me.'

The Tory election manifesto promised tax breaks worth £17.50 a week for partners of stay-at-home parents. Major said: 'Our goal must be for Britain to be the best place in the world to live.'

Labour's manifesto promised to increase the proportion of national income spent on education. Tony Blair said: 'Our case is simple: that Britain can and must be better.' The Liberal Democrat manifesto promised to cut class sizes and boost school spending, financed by a 1p increase in income tax.

Unemployed musician Noel Flanagan, wearing a Tory chicken costume to bait Blair, was attacked by Labour workers dressed as a headless chicken and two foxes in London, and had his head ripped off by a teenage girl in Stirling's shopping centre.

Blair sparked a storm in Scotland by comparing the proposed Scottish Parliament to an English parish council. The Labour campaign wobbled over unions and privatisation. Michael Heseltine claimed that Blair was 'cracking up' under pressure.

An IRA bomb scare stopped the Grand National.

Veteran TV war reporter Martin Bell stood as an anti-corruption candidate against Neil Hamilton in Tatton. Christine Hamilton said he had a 'flaming cheek'.

Labour's business manifesto drew support from bookstore mogul Tim Waterstone, Granada boss Gerry Robinson, Terence Conran and Anita Roddick.

Up to 200 Tory candidates, including minister Angela Browning, appeared to defy their party line on Europe in their election leaflets. John Prescott said: 'The Tory Party makes the Borgias look like a happy family.'

John Major said: 'They are keeping Mr Blair out of the way like he was the plague – or the New Black Death, as they would probably say.'

Tory splits over Europe re-emerged with at least 150 candidates, including vice-chairman Angela Rumbold, saying they would oppose a single currency, defying Major's 'wait and see' line.

Fitz, the British bulldog, made his debut in a Labour election broadcast.

The Tory Europe revolt swelled to more than 200 but Major refused to sack recalcitrant ministers John Horam and James Paice.

Heseltine devised an ad showing Blair as a puppet on German Chancellor Helmut Kohl's knee. Edwina Currie derided it as 'puerile', Ted Heath as 'contemptible' and Ken Clarke as 'abhorrent xenophobia'.

Writer Will Self was reported for allegedly taking heroin on Major's election plane.

Labour heavyweight David Blunkett said of his invisible guide dog, Lucy: 'She's just got fed up with press conferences and is under the table.'

Blair said: 'I am a modern man. I am part of the rock 'n' roll generation – the Beatles, colour TV. That's the generation I come from.' He unveiled a plan to use £1 billion from the midweek Lottery to fund extra education and health projects.

The Tories leaked Labour's 'war book' listing their strengths and weaknesses. Gordon Brown said: 'We are not leaking the Conservative election strategy – because there isn't one.'

SNP leader Alex Salmond said that the Queen would still reign over an independent Scotland, but only when living there.

In an ad-libbed speech, Major said: 'If I went to invade Mars, Labour would invade Mars. From their point of view, Mars today, Cadbury tomorrow and Bournville the day after.' Eh?

Labour's lead was slashed to 15 points in a rogue ICM poll, but a subsequent survey showed Labour up to 21 points ahead, hardly changed since the beginning of the election campaign. Edwina Currie predicted a Tory rout, saying: 'Our scare-mongering isn't working because it's not credible.' Another poll suggested that Labour was on course for a landslide majority of 189.

Amstrad boss Alan Sugar backed Labour, predicting he would soon be the chief executive of 'England plc'.

Stephen Dorrell accused Labour of 'bare-faced, despicable lies' over claims that the Tories would abolish the NHS. Labour refused to withdraw the allegation.

Maverick publisher Sid Shaw's Elvis Presley Party published its key election pledge: nationalise Trust House Forte and rename its hotels Heartbreak Hotels.

Lady Thatcher said: 'No-one has been able to do with Britain what we have done in the last sixteen years.' Heseltine said: 'A vote for Labour on Thursday and this country of ours will never be the same again.' He added that the country was 'sleepwalking' towards Labour. Scottish Secretary Michael Forsyth told a rally: 'Go back to your constituencies and prepare for government.' Major said: 'Soundbites butter no parsnips.' Ken Clarke said: 'I have been in parties that have lost elections and the thing to do is pick yourself up and work out how you are going to win the next one.'

'Blair's election battle bus is all fruit juice, low-fat yoghurt and cattle-prods at dawn.' – Columnist Ann Leslie.

'We are a grandfather.' – Liberal Democrat leader Paddy Ashdown.

'I am proud of my country but ashamed to see it reduced to this state.' – Tony Blair.

May
1st: Labour victory
The first handful of results confirmed a Labour landslide. Tory Cabinet ministers who lost their seats included Michael Portillo, Malcolm Rifkind, Ian Lang, William Waldegrave and Tony Newton. Former ministerial casualties included Edwina Currie, Neil Hamilton and Norman Lamont. No Conservative MPs were left in Scotland and Wales and only sixteen were left north of the Wash. It was possible to drive from John O'Groats to Land's End and only pass through one Tory constituency (Ryedale). The final

tally was: Labour 419 seats, Conservatives 165, Liberal Democrats 46, Scottish Nationalists 6, Plaid Cymru 4, Martin Bell 1, others 18 – a Labour majority of 179.

Tony Blair said at the immediate victory rally at the Festival Hall:

Well, a new dawn has broken, has it not? And it is wonderful. We have been elected as New Labour and we will govern as New Labour. The vote tonight has been a vote for the future, for a new era of politics in Britain so that we can put behind us the battles of the past century and address the challenges of the new century. We are today the people's party, the party of all the people, the many not the few, the party that belongs to every part of Britain.

On the steps of Downing Street he added: 'This New Labour government will govern in the interests of all our people – the whole of this nation. That I can promise you. It is time now to do.' Cherie Blair appeared on the doorstep of their Islington home dressed in her nightie.

John Major immediately announced he would quit as Tory leader, saying: 'When the curtain falls it's time to leave the stage.' That afternoon he took his wife Norma to the Oval to watch cricket.

*

Blair appointed his first Cabinet: Gordon Brown, Chancellor; John Prescott, deputy premier; Robin Cook, Foreign Secretary; Jack Straw, Home Secretary, George Robertson, Defence; David

Blunkett, Education; Harriet Harman, Social Security; Jack Cunningham, Agriculture; Donald Dewar, Scotland; Frank Dobson, Health; Nick Brown, Chief Whip; Mo Mowlam, Northern Ireland, Michael Meacher, Environment; Chris Smith, Heritage. More junior appointments included John Reid as armed forces minister and Tony Banks as sports minister. There were twenty-eight Scots in the government, including ministers and whips in both House. The first Cabinet meeting set an informal procedure: 'Call me Tony.'

Michael Heseltine was taken to hospital with heart trouble. The Tory leadership contest saw William Hague emerge as an early frontrunner, ahead of Ken Clarke, John Redwood, Michael Howard, Stephen Dorrell and Peter Lilley. Howard accused Hague of reneging on a deal, agreed over champagne, to stand as his deputy. Former prisons minister Ann Widdecombe said there was 'something of the night' about her ex-boss, one Michael Howard. Some days later Widdecombe accused Howard of cowardice over the sacking of former prisons boss Derek Lewis.

Robin Cook signed up to the European Social Chapter of the Maastricht Treaty, lifted the ban on trade union membership at the GCHQ intelligence-gathering centre and outlined an 'ethical' foreign policy, saying: 'The government does not believe that political values can be left behind when we check in our passports.'

Blair told Labour MPs: 'We are not the masters now, we are the servants.'

In the Queen's Speech, devolution topped the list of twenty-six Bills. A blanket ban on all handguns was promised, Straw launched an inquiry into the sale of alcopops, and MI5 advertised for recruits.

Hague denounced the 'constantly shifting fudge' of the Major years.

Mowlam, undergoing chemotherapy for cancer, took off her wig at a press conference.

Bill and Hillary Clinton enjoyed a day's love-in with Tony and Cherie Blair.

The government announced that up to 800,000 jobless single parents with children at school would be called into Jobcentres to encourage them to find work. Blair said it was part of his drive to end the blight of Britain's 'workless class'.

Camelot's top four directors awarded themselves pay rises of between 40 and 90 per cent despite a fall in Lottery ticket sales, standing to share around £2 million, including bonuses. Chris Smith condemned 'profiteering'. In a compromise deal the directors agreed to donate a proportion of future bonuses to charity.

'Ours is the first generation able to contemplate the possibility that we may live our entire lives without going to war or sending our children to war.' – Tony Blair.

June

Joan Ruddock was appointed minister for women ... at no extra salary.

Films minister Tom Clarke said that one of his favourite movie moments was the farting scene in *Blazing Saddles*.

Ken Clarke topped the Tory leadership first ballot, but Peter Lilley and Michael Howard dropped out, urging their supporters to back William Hague. John Redwood dropped out after the second ballot and urged his supporters to back Clarke in return for a promise of the shadow Chancellorship. They rejected that deal and Hague was elected leader – the youngest for 212 years – by 92 votes to 70. Clarke retired from frontline politics.

Disgraced former Tory Cabinet minister Jonathan Aitken was forced to drop a libel action following evidence that he lied to the High Court about an alleged freebie at the Paris Ritz. *Guardian* editor Alan Rusbridger said he had 'impaled himself on the sword of truth'. Aitken was left with a £1.8 million legal bill.

Army surplus tents sprayed with organophosphates during the Gulf War had been sold to the Boy Scouts, it was revealed.

Blair put Peter Mandelson in charge of the Millennium Dome project. He renamed it the Millennium Experience and justified spiralling costs by saying: 'Millenniums come but once every thousand years.'

Blair attacked American environmental policy after arriving at a summit in Denver on Concorde.

Jack Straw announced a new inquiry into the Hillsborough football disaster.

At midnight on 30 June Hong Kong was handed back to China. Prince Charles said: 'We shall not forget you and we shall watch with the closest interest as you embark on this new era in your remarkable history.'

July

Gordon Brown's first Budget included a tax on windfall earnings, a cut in corporation tax, home fuel VAT reduced to 5 per cent, 19p a packet on cigarettes, 4p a litre on petrol, £1.3 billion more for schools. Tony Blair said to William Hague after the Budget debate: 'My advice is to quit while you're behind.'

An inquiry by Sir Gordon Downey found Neil Hamilton guilty of taking up to £25,000 in brown envelopes from Mohammed al-Fayed, and implicated four other senior Tories – Tim Smith, Sir Michael Grylls, Sir Andrew Bowden and Michael Brown.

Mo Mowlam allowed the Orange Order to march through the Catholic enclave of Drumcree. That was followed by widespread rioting, fire-bombings and shootings, with nationalists claiming they had been betrayed.

A report from Lord Nolan into sleaze recommended a new

crime of misusing public office, which would cover ministers, MPs, civil servants and councillors.

The cost of flying Cherie Blair's favourite hairdresser to the Denver summit was revealed to be £2,000, which she paid herself.

An estimated 100,000 gathered in Hyde Park to oppose a proposed ban on fox-hunting.

The government announced that the age of consent for gay sex was to be cut to sixteen . . . but the minimum age for smoking would be raised to eighteen.

On the 19th the IRA declared a ceasefire. Ministers agreed that if it held for six weeks, Sinn Fein would be able to join cross-party peace talks. An independent body would be set up to oversee the decommissioning of paramilitary weapons.

Education Secretary David Blunkett announced the introduction of £1,000-a-year university tuition fees. Stephen Dorrell described it as 'a shabby, opportunistic, smash-and-grab raid on low-income families'.

Scottish Secretary Donald Dewar unveiled a historic White Paper on plans for a Scottish Parliament, and urged the Scots to vote in the upcoming referendum for both devolution and tax-raising powers. 'Make mine a double,' he said.

Robin Cook gave the go-ahead to the sale of Hawk jets to

Indonesia, despite evidence that they would be used to crush domestic dissidents.

Paisley Labour MP Gordon McMaster was found dead in his garage, four days after committing suicide. In a letter he blamed colleagues for orchestrating a smear campaign against him. He said: 'I expect to go to heaven. I don't expect to see them there. If so, I hope it's in a dark alley.'

Labour lost the Uxbridge by-election. William Hague said: 'We are back in business.'

August

New Labour peers included film producer David Puttnam, crime writer Ruth Rendell and supermarket mogul David Sainsbury.

Robin Cook left Margaret, his wife of twenty-eight years, for his secretary, Gaynor Regan, saying the marital break-up was entirely his own fault. It emerged that No. 10's media chief, Alastair Campbell, had called him en route to an airport with Margaret, and told him the *News of the World* had film of him walking out of Gaynor's flat. He cancelled the holiday, telling his wife in the departure lounge, and chose Gaynor. Tony Blair sent Margaret a 'wish you well' message.

'Nobody bleeps me, I do all the bleeping,' said Peter Mandelson when asked to turn off his pager before a TV interview. He then unveiled a new task force, to be chaired by Blair, to tackle the problems of the underclass.

Labour backbencher Tommy Graham was suspended pending an inquiry into west of Scotland politics. Chief whip Nick Brown cleared him of responsibility for Gordon McMaster's death but found 'good reason' for a further probe into claims of bringing the party into disrepute.

John Prescott forecast the end of the two-car family.

Princess Diana, in an interview with a French magazine on land-mines, said that the previous Tory government was 'hopeless'.

Actress Joan Collins said that William Hague looked like a 'foetus'.

Mo Mowlam was convinced that the IRA ceasefire was genuine and invited Sinn Fein to join all-party talks. Chief negotiator Martin McGuinness said it was 'the most wonderful opportunity we will have this century to bring about a settlement'.

On the last evening of the month Princess Diana and her boyfriend Dodi Fayed were killed in a car crash in Paris while their Mercedes was being pursued by paparazzi.

September
Most political activity, including the Scottish referendum campaign, was suspended as Diana's body was flown to Britain. The media were initially blamed for hounding the princess to her death, but criticism was muted when it was revealed that her driver, who also died, was over the drink-drive limit and was driving at 120mph through the centre of Paris. Public anger

switched to the Queen and the Royal Family, perceived as cold, aloof and hiding behind protocol. The initial plan for a private funeral was overturned, although it was several days before the flag was flown at half mast over Buckingham Palace. Tony Blair stepped in, dubbed Diana 'the People's Princess' and persuaded the Queen to return from Balmoral for a state funeral in Westminster Abbey.

Scotland voted 3-1 for a Scottish Parliament and 2-1 in favour of tax-varying powers. Donald Dewar was given the credit for a superb campaign.

A week later Wales voted by the narrowest of margins – 0.6 per cent, or just 6,000 votes – for an Assembly. Welsh Secretary Ron Davies said the result was 'stunning'.

In Northern Ireland, unionists and republicans agreed to face-to-face peace talks. Mo Mowlam said: 'We have broken through but it is not going to be easy.'

Liberal Democrat leader Paddy Ashdown told his party conference that they must 'get real' and co-operate with Labour. Disgraced former leader Jeremy Thorpe received a standing ovation by appearing at his first conference in twenty years.

At the Labour conference in Brighton John Prescott said he had been told not to be triumphalist and added: 'Sod it, we won.' Blair promised that Britain can be 'simply the best'. He announced an extra £2 billion to repair crumbling schools and connect every pupil to the internet. Potential revolts over

Railtrack, tuition fees and party reform were bought off. Peter Mandelson was beaten by ex-GLC chief Ken Livingstone for a seat on the party's executive.

October

At the Tory conference William Hague repackaged his party as 'compassionate, tolerant and principled' while assuring the old guard that he would not ditch commitments to the family and free enterprise. Michael Portillo confessed that the Tories were seen as arrogant and conceited and urged the party to look more kindly on single mothers and gays. Lord Tebbit was ostracised for an attack on Britain's multicultural society.

Piers Merchant quit as Tory MP for Beckenham after claims of a renewed affair with ex-Soho hostess Anna Cox.

Gordon Brown and his spin doctors were blamed for uncertainty over European monetary union, which wiped nearly £20 billion off share prices. He was forced to issue a statement backing a single currency in principle but effectively ruling it out for five years. Tory turmoil over Europe continued.

Hague hosted a bonding session for Tory MPs in Eastbourne. It ended in a sing-song but no-one knew the words to the Oasis hit 'Don't Look Back in Anger'. They sang 'We Shall Overcome' instead.

November

The government exempted Formula One motor racing from a proposed ban on tobacco advertising in sport. It emerged that health minister Tessa Jowell's husband, a lawyer, was acting on behalf of a racing company. She insisted: 'No conflict of interest.' Blair was then engulfed in a sleaze row when it was confirmed that Formula One boss Bernie Ecclestone had donated £1 million to Labour before a meeting with Blair to press for the exemption. Labour promised to return the cash. Martin Bell asked: 'Have we slain one dragon only to have another take its place with a red rose in its mouth?' No. 10 became known as the 'Berni Inn'.

Labour's Douglas Alexander won the Paisley South by-election but with a majority slashed from almost 13,000 to 2,731.

Blair ordered the Ministry of Defence to apologise after a tattered Union flag was flown upside down at the Remembrance Day parade.

Blair appointed the late princess's butler, Paul Burrell, to the Diana Memorial Committee. John Major was appointed 'guardian' to Princes William and Harry to help sort out Diana's legacy.

Humphrey, the Downing Street cat, was taken away for retirement suffering a kidney complaint, sparking rumours that he had been put down on the orders of Cherie Blair. No. 10 said: 'He is in a quiet, suburban place . . . no, not a cemetery.' A photo-call in a secret location was arranged.

MPs voted 411-151 to ban fox-hunting with hounds.

Treasury minister Geoffrey Robinson could benefit from a

£12.5 million offshore trust fund, it was claimed. He faced increasing pressure to resign after admitting he had played a role in business deals by a tax-free Guernsey trust.

'I can't bear all this touchy-feely stuff.' – Gordon Brown.

December

Agriculture Minister Jack Cunningham announced a ban on all beef on the bone. Protesters dumped tons of imported Irish beef. Later he declared a ban effective from 1 January on meat imports which did not meet British safety standards.

Lauren Booth, half-sister of Cherie Blair, said: 'I watched my charming Marmite sandwich-making brother-in-law change before my eyes into our leader.'

Scottish minister Malcolm Chisholm quit ahead of a vote on cuts to single mothers' benefits. Forty-seven Labour MPs rebelled on the issue. Among them were several ministerial aides including Alice Mahon, who, referring to Labour's election anthem 'Things Can Only Get Better', said: 'I think I missed the verse on lone parents.'

Sinn Fein's Gerry Adams met Blair in Downing Street. The PM told him: 'It is important that I can look you in the eye and hear you say you are committed to peace.' Adams replied: 'All of us in this process have to take risks for peace.' Loyalist terrorist Billy Wright, known as King Rat, was shot dead by INLA terrorists inside the Maze prison. A republican doorman was slain in a tit-for-tat killing.

The Blair Decade

Donald Dewar published the Scotland Bill in Glasgow while his civil servants were stuck on a snow-bound train at Carlisle.

William Hague married civil servant Ffion Jenkins in the crypt at the Palace of Westminster.

Blair began moves to abolish Lords seats for hereditary peers.

1998

The historic Good Friday peace agreement was followed by Northern Ireland's worst atrocity, while sleaze and incompetence took their toll on Blair's ministerial line-up.

January

Elton John was knighted in the New Year Honours list. 'Elton's already a queen, isn't this a bit of a comedown?' said Boy George. Other awards went to Deborah Kerr, Petula Clark and veteran footballer Tom Finney.

One person was killed and five wounded when loyalist terrorists machine-gunned a bar in continuing revenge attacks for the murder of Billy Wright.

Scottish newspapers revealed that a seventeen-year-old called William Straw, alleged to be a drug dealer, was the son of Home Secretary Jack Straw. The story was off limits to the English press until the High Court lifted a gagging order. The teenager was later given a police caution, having sold a small amount of cannabis to an undercover reporter.

Peter Mandelson flew to Walt Disney World in Florida to pick up tips for the Millennium Dome.

On the search for a new symbol for post-Communist Russia, *Izvestia* commented: 'Perhaps it is time to replace the old hammer and sickle with the gun and vodka bottle, symbols of murder and drunkenness.'

Donald Dewar announced that he was to stand as Scotland's First Minister.

Northern Ireland Secretary Mo Mowlam gambled on meeting both loyalist and IRA convicted terrorists in the Maze prison. She persuaded Protestant paramilitaries to drop their opposition to peace talks, reopened the peace process and preserved the three-year-old loyalist ceasefire.

Margaret Cook claimed that her estranged husband Robin had had 'several affairs' during their marriage, that it ended when Cook spoke to Downing Street as they set off on a riding holiday in Nevada (she had packed a surprise gift of leather chaps), and that Cook had a 'super-shiny ego'. She also claimed that he had collapsed in a hotel room in 1987 after drinking a bottle of brandy. Cook announced he was seeking a divorce to marry Gaynor Regan. Blair vetoed Cook taking her on a round-the-world official trip.

Labour Party debt topped £4.5 million.

Blair, while in Tokyo, brokered a 'breakthrough' in the Northern

Ireland peace process. All the main parties agreed to negotiate a blueprint which included an assembly, an inter-governmental council and a north–south ministerial council to oversee Ireland-wide co-operation on economic, trade and other issues.

Ministers confirmed that welfare reforms could see all state benefits means tested. Measures expected included axing universal child benefit for teenage mothers, a two-tier pension plan and cuts in maternity pay for better-off women.

A spat erupted over journalist Paul Routledge's 'authorised' biography of Gordon Brown, which suggested the Chancellor still believed that Blair reneged on a deal which would have put Brown in No. 10.

February

Tit-for-tat killings continued in Northern Ireland, with five murders in one week. Protestant paramilitaries admitted to breaching the ceasefire, saying their murders were a 'measured response'.

'Mr Clean' Martin Bell, denying any wrong-doing, repaid £9,600 in undeclared legal fees paid by Labour and the Liberal Democrats during the previous year's contest, in breach of electoral law.

School standards minister Stephen Byers, quizzed in a radio show, reckoned that eight sevens came to fifty-four.

Robin Cook denied claims that he sacked his Foreign Office diary secretary, Anne Bullen, in a failed bid to install Gaynor Regan.

The Blair Decade

John Major, while on holiday, said: 'I would like to thank the British electorate for giving me the opportunity to watch cricket in the West Indies for the first time.' Play was stopped after fifty minutes.

William Hague on Peter Mandelson's recent visit to Walt Disney World: 'Peter shook hands with Mickey Mouse and noticed he was wearing a Harriet Harman watch.'

Lord Chancellor Lord Irvine suggested the Human Rights Bill could be used to gag the press over politicians' private lives.

Tony Blair told President Bill Clinton at a Washington summit: 'I am proud to call you a good friend.' The press conference was dominated by sex allegations involving former White House intern Monica Lewinsky.

Bob Hope was given an honorary knighthood.

Blair banned most ministers from accepting World Cup tickets and freebies.

Danbert Nobacon – previously Nigel Hunter – of the anarchist pop group Chumbawamba poured a bucket of iced water over John Prescott at the Brit awards. The deputy premier branded the attack 'cowardly'.

Enoch Powell died, aged 85. His body was allowed to lie in Westminster Abbey.

Blair appointed his old English teacher, Eric Anderson, chairman of the National Heritage Memorial Fund.

The cost to the taxpayer of household items in Lord Irvine's refurbished House of Lords apartment was revealed to be £239,000. That included £25,000 for a table, two beds costing up to £10,000, £58,000 for wallpaper and curtains at £200 a metre. He also borrowed eighty-seven works of art worth £1 million. Overall the refurbishment cost £650,000, it was later revealed. Irvine told a select committee that it was a 'noble cause'. He added: 'We are talking about quality materials which are capable of lasting sixty or seventy years. We are not talking about something down in a DIY store which may collapse after a year or two.'

Donald Dewar vetoed a knighthood for Sean Connery because, it was claimed, the former James Bond backed the Scottish National Party.

Saddam Hussein and UN secretary general Kofi Annan agreed a compromise which averted Anglo-American air strikes on Iraq. Both Blair and Clinton made it clear that they didn't trust the dictator to honour the deal. Forces remained on standby in the region. Annan said: 'You can do a lot with diplomacy, but of course you can do a lot more with diplomacy backed up by fairness and force.'

March
The Scottish Labour conference at Perth condemned lone parent benefit cuts as 'economically inept, morally repugnant and spiritually bereft'.

Gordon Brown's Budget included:
- A guarantee to every family of at least £180 a week, with no income tax paid on earnings under £200 a week.
- An extra £500 million for the NHS, £250 million for education.
- A freeze on spirits duty, 1p on a pint of beer, 4p on a bottle of wine, 21p on cigarettes, 4.5p on a litre of petrol, but road tax on smaller-engined cars cut from £150 to £100.
- A record rise in child benefit – up £2.50 for the first child for all, and up another £2.50 for under-elevens in families on income support.

Brown called it a Budget 'for the family'.

Welfare minister Frank Field published a Green Paper on reform, including a blitz on housing benefit cheats, compulsory second pensions to top up the state handout, stiffer tests for incapacity benefits, reform of the Child Support Agency, and insurance policies to cover sickness and unemployment.

Tory MP Sir Tony Fell and veteran Labourites Joan Lestor and Joan Maynard died.

April
The discovery of a thousand-pound bomb and a clash over the powers of the proposed all-Ireland administrative body threatened to wreck the Northern Ireland peace process. A series of meetings in London between Tony Blair and Irish premier Bertie Ahern saved it from collapse. A 9 April deadline drew close.

Robin Cook married Gaynor Regan in secret – at Tunbridge Wells register office, in the pouring rain and a green anorak.

10th: Good Friday

A historic peace settlement was thrashed out after a marathon all-night and all-day session of the cross-party talks in Stormont. Gerry Adams told the meeting: 'We've brought a camp bed. We don't share it, of course.' The key points were: a 108-member Northern Ireland Assembly to take over the day-to-day running of the province, headed by a twelve-strong executive with members from all main parties; a north–south council, with Belfast and Dublin representatives, to consult on matters of common interest; a Council of the Isles to cement links between the Republic and different parts of the UK. The Irish Republic amended its constitutional claim to all Ireland. British law was changed so that Northern Ireland could leave the UK, but only by a majority vote. Referendums in Northern Ireland and the Republic were set for 22 May. Blair said: 'The burden of history can at long last start to be lifted from our shoulders.' Ahern said: 'Today is about the promise of a bright future – a day when we hope a line can be drawn under the bloody past.' Since 1968 more than 3,600 people had died in the Troubles.

The Irish government released nine IRA prisoners. The Orange Order and the Democratic Unionists rejected the peace agreement. Gordon Brown signalled a £200 million aid package if the people of Northern Ireland and the Republic agreed the deal. The ruling council of the Ulster Unionists voted over-whelmingly to back the agreement under a deal put to them by David Trimble. Gerry Adams said: 'Well done, David.' Blair said:

'This is not a day for soundbites . . . I feel the hand of history on my shoulder.'

*

Elsewhere, the comedian Ben Elton said: 'I can do without the Labour Party trying to strut its funny stuff.' The impressionist Rory Bremner said: 'Doing Tony Blair was definitely difficult at first, but he is getting so messianic now it is a lot easier.' International Development Secretary Clare Short said: 'In opposition I found toadying Tories creepy. I wouldn't have expected Labour MPs to be the same, but they are.'

Paymaster-General Geoffrey Robinson was accused of a 25-year affair with Italian actress Annabella Incontrera.

John Prescott test drove a prototype solar-powered car – and crashed it into a taxi.

'If I ever left the House of Commons it would be because I wanted to spend more time in politics.' – Tony Benn.

May

Robin Cook denied that Foreign Office ministers knew of illegal supplies of arms and mercenaries sent into Sierra Leone by the British firm Sandline to topple that country's dictator. A criminal inquiry was launched, sparking the arms-for-Africa outcry. Cook was reportedly furious at claims that he tried to shift blame to junior minister Tony Lloyd. Blair described the whole affair as a 'hoo-ha'.

The G8 summit in Birmingham saw the US President having fish and chips in a canalside pub. Local pensioner Mavis Stone said: 'I nearly choked on my tuna salad when Bill Clinton drew up a chair and sat at the table next to me.'

Michael Stone, who had carried out the Milltown Cemetery murders ten years earlier, was granted early release as part of the Northern Ireland peace accord. On 22 May Northern Ireland voted for a peace deal by a margin of 71 per cent to 29 per cent. In the Republic the 'yes' vote was higher – 94.4 per cent to 5.6 per cent. Mo Mowlam said: 'They have voted to take the gun out of politics.' Blair said: 'A day of joy. The electorate has shown courage and vision.' An independent decommissioning body offered safeguards for handing in terrorist arms, including an amnesty for crimes involving those weapons. A row erupted when Gerry Adams and Martin McGuinness were invited to a royal garden party in Belfast hosted by Prince Charles, and refused to attend.

The Low Pay Commission recommended a national minimum wage of £3.60 an hour for people aged over twenty-one, £3.20 for 18–20-year-olds.

Japanese Emperor Akihito refused to make a full apology for the Second World War treatment of British prisoners of war, saying only that he was sorry for the suffering the war inflicted on all sides. Veterans turned their back on him when he went to receive the Order of the Garter – Britain's highest chivalric honour – from the Queen.

June
Pakistan exploded six nuclear devices in retaliation for India's

earlier testing. Bill Clinton said: 'I cannot believe we are about to start the twenty-first century with the Indian subcontinent repeating the worst mistakes of the twentieth.'

The Rolling Stones cancelled the British leg of their world tour after claiming that Budget changes would cost them £12 million in tax if they appeared on stage.

Gordon Brown unveiled public–private partnerships, which the left saw as back-door privatisation, to run air traffic control, the Tote, the Royal Mint and other public assets. He also announced that public spending rises were to be kept to 2.25 per cent in a three-year period of restraint.

The Tories joined the Ulster Unionists in voting against the Northern Ireland Assembly Bill in protest at an alleged failure to link the early release of paramilitary prisoners with arms decommissioning.

A new batch of Labour working life peers included the arts broadcaster Melvyn Bragg and Northern Food chairman Christopher Haskins, credited with inventing the ready-made meal.

MPs voted to lower the age of consent for gay sex from eighteen to sixteen.

The Northern Ireland Assembly elections left Official Unionist David Trimble leading the biggest party, with surges for both John Hume's Social Democratic and Labour Party and Ian

Paisley's Democratic Unionist Party. Dissident Unionists narrowly failed to win enough seats to block co-operation between unionists and nationalists.

July

David Trimble was elected First Minister in the first session of the new Assembly. The Parades Commission vetoed the Orange Lodge march at Drumcree, a traditional violent flashpoint. Barbed wire and armoured cars blocked the way. Loyalists rioted and burnt Catholic churches.

William Hague had an operation for sinusitis.

No. 10 advisor Roger Liddle and former Peter Mandelson aide turned lobbyist Derek Draper were accused of offering insider help to businessmen in a cash-for-access row. Downing Street denied any impropriety. Hague accused Tony Blair of surrounding himself with 'money-grubbing, feather-bedding, pocket-lining cronies'. Cabinet Secretary Sir Richard Wilson was told to update the code of conduct. Blair said he expected his people to be 'whiter than white'. Draper left Westminster to become a psychologist in California.

Gordon Brown's comprehensive spending review included an extra £57 billion over the next three years, with £19 million going to education and £21 billion to the NHS. Health Secretary Frank Dobson pledged 15,000 extra nurses and 7,000 more doctors.

John Prescott announced plans to introduce motorway and inner city road tolls to avoid gridlock. He said: 'The anti-car policy would be to do nothing.' Later in the month he cut the road-building budget from £6 billion to £1.4 billion, axing 100 proposed schemes.

Jack Straw unveiled a £3.8 billion blitz on youth crime and Hilary Armstrong announced a £3.6 billion programme to renovate run-down council estates, using council house sale receipts unfrozen by the Chancellor.

Armed forces minister John Reid stopped short of a full posthumous pardon for 306 British soldiers executed in the First World War, but urged that their names be added to regimental rolls of honour. He also abolished the death penalty under military law.

Blair's first Cabinet reshuffle saw Peter Mandelson as Trade and Industry Secretary, Stephen Byers as Chief Secretary to the Treasury, Alistair Darling in charge of Social Security, John Reid as transport minister and Nick Brown as Agriculture Minister. Jack Cunningham became the Cabinet's policy 'enforcer', a role originally earmarked for Mandelson. Baroness Jay became Leader of the Lords, Margaret Beckett Leader of the Commons, and Ann Taylor the first-ever female chief whip. Harriet Harman was sacked as Social Security Secretary and left her department with a bunch of white lilies and a handbag presented by staff. Frank Field, the minister told to think the unthinkable about welfare reforms, quit when he was not offered Harman's job. He blamed Harman and Gordon Brown for blocking his reforms. Middle-ranking ministers were among many other casualties, swelling the ranks of the disaffected and disappointed on the back benches.

In a second wave Lord Falconer, barrister pal of the Blairs, became minister without portfolio, Lord Sainsbury joined the DTI, Charles Clarke and Margaret Hodge went to Education, Patricia Hewitt became economic secretary to the Treasury, John Denham became Darling's deputy and Alan Meale joined Prescott's Department of Environment, Transport and the Regions.

Defence Secretary George Robertson decreed that British soldiers would not lay landmines.

Derek Bentley finally won a posthumous reprieve forty-six years after he was hanged for a murder actually committed by a friend.

Straw outlined proposals which could mean that defendants would lose their rights to a trial by jury.

Cook blamed a breakdown in communication between diplomats and ministers for the arms-to-Africa scandal.

MI5 revealed that it held files on nearly 500,000 people but insisted that only 20,000 of them – including 13,000 on UK citizens – were active.

Blair published the annual report of 'Great Britain plc' under Labour.

'When I was Prime Minister, I was not always popular.' – Lady Thatcher.

August

Scottish Media Group chairman Gus Macdonald was made Scottish industry minister with the promise of a peerage, sparking opposition claims of cronyism.

Whistleblower David Shayler, a former MI5 officer, was arrested. He claimed that MI6 had plotted to kill Libya's Colonel Gaddafi.

Frank Dobson insisted that nursing pay must be increased to solve staff shortages.

Frank Field said that spin doctors are a 'cancer' at the heart of government.

Islamic terrorists bombed US embassies in Nairobi and Dar es Salaam, killing 257 people: twelve Americans, the rest Africans.

A milk health scare erupted after a report linked cattle disease to a painful stomach complaint. The government refused to ban genetically modified food after research suggesting it could damage human immune systems was found to be faulty.

15th: in Omagh, Northern Ireland's worst-ever bombing claimed twenty-eight lives, nine of them children, including an eighteen-month-old baby. Most of the rest, plus 200 injured, were women doing their weekly shop. A bogus warning sent them into a trap. Tony Blair said: 'So much of our emotions are grief but there has to be with that grief the determination that these people won't win, that they are not going to destroy the chance of a decent future for the people of Northern Ireland.' Gerry Adams condemned the outrage 'without any equivocation whatsoever'. Bertie Ahern said: 'This is the most evil deed in years.' RUC chief constable Ronnie Flanagan said: 'We have had men, women and children slaughtered here by murderers who have nothing else to offer.' David Trimble said: 'This would not have happened had the IRA already handed in its weapons.' The breakaway 'Real IRA' claimed responsibility and then announced its own ceasefire. Ahern unveiled a draconian crackdown on terrorist groups in the Republic. Blair visited Omagh and recalled Parliament to drive through new anti-terror laws, including powers to convict for membership of an illegal organisation on the say-so of a police superintendent.

Lady Thatcher revealed that she was going deaf, Denis couldn't play golf and Labour would win the next election.

September

Gerry Adams said that the war was over, that Sinn Fein was committed to 'making conflict a thing of the past, over, done with and gone'. Martin McGuinness agreed to liaise with the Independent International Commission on Decommissioning. Both Houses of Parliament were recalled for two days to push through the anti-terror Bill, which included the seizure of property used in terrorism and a new offence of conspiracy to commit offences abroad. The Bill received Royal Assent after an all-night sitting. Later, Adams said of David Trimble that he was 'a man I can do business with'.

Rupert Murdoch's BSkyB put in a £625 million bid for Manchester United.

Glasgow Labour MP Tommy Graham was expelled from the party after a fourteen-month inquiry found him guilty of smearing colleagues. He said: 'This is not the end of Tommy,' before going to the pub.

The electronics firm Fujitsu announced almost 600 job losses in Tony Blair's Sedgefield constituency. He said he could not protect jobs from the 'twists and turns of the world markets'.

Frank Dobson ruled that Viagra would not be prescribed on the NHS.

Peter Mandelson promised the TUC: 'No grandstanding, no playing to the gallery, no spin . . . honest.' TUC president John Edmonds called fat-cat directors who award themselves big rises 'greedy bastards'.

David Blunkett unveiled a new literacy campaign using TV soaps.

The government announced that pet passports would be issued alongside a relaxation of the quarantine laws.

The Liberal Democrat conference debated the party's relationship with Labour.

Blair told his party conference that there could be no let-up in the pace of reform.

Prescott promised tougher regulation of the rail network, saying: 'I'm no Virgin.'

October

At the Tory conference William Hague won 84 per cent backing for his policy of resisting the euro for at least eight years. A *Sun* front page depicted him as a dead parrot hanging upside down from his perch.

Lord Neill unveiled proposals to regulate party funding, including a ban on foreign donations and a £20 million cap on election campaigns.

Former Chilean dictator General Augusto Pinochet was arrested in a London clinic as Britain received an extradition bid from Spain.

Alistair Darling unveiled a welfare Bill to force benefit claimants to show they are actively seeking work. Lady Thatcher said that single mothers should be cared for in religious institutions or by charities.

Bank of England governor Eddie George said that job losses in the north were acceptable as a price for curbing inflation in the south.

President Carlos Menem of Argentina visited Britain. An article in which he appeared to apologise for the Falklands invasion was written, it was claimed, by Alastair Campbell.

Ron Davies quit as Welsh Secretary and would-be First Minister after he was robbed having picked up a stranger on Clapham Common, a haunt of gay prostitutes and drug dealers. He confessed to a 'serious error of judgement' and a 'moment of madness.' He left his wife and resigned as an MP.

Peter Mandelson referred BSkyB's bid for Manchester United to the Monopolies and Mergers Commission. He was outed as gay by former Tory MP turned commentator Matthew Parris.

'Paddy Ashdown is the only party leader who is a trained killer. Although, to be fair, Mrs Thatcher was self-taught.' – Charles Kennedy.

'The more battered, the more careworn, the better.' – artist Peter Howson on why he would like to paint Robin Cook.

November

Gordon Brown's pre-Budget report allowed pensioners to earn more before paying income tax and extended childcare tax credits to all children up to the age of fourteen.

Agriculture minister Nick Brown came out as gay after hearing that newspapers planned to run a story about a two-year affair with a young man. The *Sun* asked if Britain was run by a 'gay Mafia', then in a U-turn pledged to stop irrelevant outings. Tony Blair stood by Brown. John Prescott slammed the media for being 'judge, jury and executioner' in the outing of gays.

Scottish Labourite Dennis Canavan branded Blair a 'control freak' with Stalinist tendencies. Fellow left-winger Ken Livingstone condemned a selection process which seemed designed to stop him standing as Labour's candidate for London mayor. In Wales, apparent efforts to prevent Rhodri Morgan standing as First Minister were doomed – Morgan was regarded by Downing Street as too much his own man.

Blair announced closer co-operation with the Liberal Democrats to end the 'tribalism' of British politics.

Blair and Bill Clinton authorised air strikes against Saddam Hussein for blocking UN inspectors. US missiles were locked onto their targets and RAF Tornados were about to take off when Saddam backed down.

Education minister Estelle Morris said that pupils found with cannabis should not be automatically expelled.

All animal testing for cosmetics was banned.

The Scotland Bill to set up an elected Parliament north of the border received Royal Assent.

The Queen's Speech outlined Bills to abolish the voting and sitting rights of hereditary peers, introduce closed lists for European elections, require all benefit claimants to attend interviews, lower the gay age of consent to sixteen, restore union rights after workplace ballots, permit private security firms to collar fine-dodgers, and scrap GP fundholding and the NHS internal market.

The European Union ban on UK beef exports was lifted after thirty-two months of scares surrounding BSE and CJD, which cost £4.6 billion.

December

William Hague sacked Lord Cranborne, the Tory leader in the Lords, for brokering a deal with the government to keep ninety-one hereditary peers in the first phase of reform of the Upper House. Hague stuck to the deal anyway, however.

Jack Straw ruled that General Pinochet must face a court hearing on extradition, but that was overturned on appeal.

Clare Short said she would not act like a second-hand car saleswoman.

In Operation Desert Fox Tony Blair and Bill Clinton launched four days of air strikes against Saddam's arsenal. Blair claimed that Saddam had been put back 'in his cage'. But the raids sparked international condemnation and claims that they were a diversion from bids to impeach Clinton over the Lewinsky affair.

Peter Mandelson and Paymaster-General Geoffrey Robinson resigned after it was disclosed that Robinson had given Mandelson a £370,000 low-interest home loan, which he had not declared, for a fashionable Notting Hill flat. Blair said it was a 'personal tragedy'. In the subsequent reshuffle Stephen Byers replaced Mandelson, Alan Milburn replaced Byers and Geoff Hoon replaced Robinson. The row continued over claims that Mandelson took free flights from an American underwear tycoon.

1999

Blair went to war in the former Yugoslavia, while at home the agenda was dominated by Northern Ireland, House of Lords reform, devolution and increasingly rebellious backbenchers.

January

Tony Blair 'saved' a Danish tourist from drowning in the Seychelles, but dentist Hans Joergensen denied that he was in difficulty.

Stephen Byers revealed that he had had a child when he was seventeen.

Gordon Brown's advisor Charlie Whelan quit to be a chat show host, saying: 'I've had job offers from City firms which would make me enough to pay off Peter Mandelson's mortgage.'

Officials claimed that Cabinet enforcer Jack Cunningham flew to America on Concorde, stayed in a five-star hotel and sipped malt at £7.60 a shot – all at the taxpayers' expense. It emerged that since coming to power ministers had spent more than £11 million on travel. John Prescott's first trip to India cost £99,000, followed by other lavish visits to Rio de Janeiro, São Paolo, Miami and Washington. A 1997 trip to the Far East with Robin Cook and fourteen officials cost almost £170,000.

Donald Dewar published plans for a non-confrontational, horseshoe chamber in the new Scottish Parliament.

Paddy Ashdown announced that he would quit as Liberal Democrat leader in June and as an MP at the next election. He said: 'Too many party leaders get carried out or kicked out.'

The government began to scrap the political power of hereditary peers, setting up a royal commission under Lord Wakeham to consider long-term reform. Hereditaries would also lose free parking and the use of restaurants at Westminster.

Tory ex-minister Jonathan Aitken pleaded guilty to perjury. Facing a prison sentence, he said he would cope, as he'd been to Eton. Later he was sentenced to eighteen months.

Lady Thatcher said that Blair was 'bossy', while an unnamed Whitehall mandarin said that Gordon Brown had the social skills of 'a whelk'.

February
Dame Edna Everage declared she was renouncing her title, saying: 'My mother would turn in her grave, if she was dead.'

Spain and Britain clashed over Gibraltar after the Spanish refused to let those with Gibraltarian driving licences cross the border.

Jack Straw proposed that psychopaths might be locked up even if they had not committed a crime. He then slapped a gagging order on leaked extracts from the report into the murder of black teenager Stephen Lawrence, which showed 'institutional racism' in the Metropolitan Police. He was forced to back down and the published report showed massive incompetence during the course of the murder investigation. Straw refused to sack Metropolitan Police commissioner Sir Paul Condon. The report's appendices named forty-seven informers. Straw went missing, leaving a junior minister to make a Commons statement about that blunder.

Science minister Lord Sainsbury refused to resign over his links with the food industry. Blair said he eats the stuff.

Ulster Unionists refused to sit with Sinn Fein in a Northern Ireland Assembly until the IRA began decommissioning.

Blair launched a national changeover plan to prepare Britain for a single currency.

March
Prince Charles and Welsh Secretary Alun Michael tasted government-banned beef on the bone at a meat presentation.

The United States opened a banana war with the European Union, including a ban on Scottish cashmere.

Gordon Brown's Budget included 1p off the basic rate of income tax from April 2000; a children's tax credit to replace the married couple's allowance; an increase in pensioners' winter fuel allowance from £20 to £100; a £60-a-week credit for over-fifties moving off welfare into jobs; an extra £1.1 billion for schools, hospitals and crime prevention; 17.5p on twenty cigarettes (but nothing on alcohol); 3.8p on a litre of leaded petrol; and an increase in the national insurance threshold to help 900,000 workers.

David Blunkett's guide dog, Lucy, vomited in the Commons chamber.

Labour MP Joe Ashton was found doing 'nothing illegal' in a Thai brothel.

European President Jacques Santer and all twenty European Commissioners resigned after a report exposed cronyism and their failure to curb corruption. French Commissioner Edith Cresson, who gave her dentist a job, said: 'I regret nothing.'

In Northern Ireland, republican civil rights lawyer Rosemary Nelson was murdered by loyalist terrorists. Loyalist Frankie Curry was also shot dead, apparently by the same group.

'If you don't leave my boy alone, I'll box your ears.' – John Prescott's mother, Phyllis Swale, to critics of his coral-diving jaunt in India.

Robin Cook was the target of an elaborate smear campaign wrongly alleging he asked officials to investigate the private life of arch-critic Diane Abbott.

The Law Lords ruled that General Pinochet could be extradited to Spain but left the final decision to Jack Straw. Lady Thatcher visited 'my friend' Pinochet for a well-publicised tea.

Operation Allied Strike: Britain joined a NATO blitz on Serbian positions to halt massacres and the oppression of ethnic Albanians in Kosovo. Serb leader Slobodan Milošević declared war on NATO. Up to 400 warplanes, including eight British Harriers, launched waves of bomb and missile attacks. There were reports of Serbians using civilians as human shields. Most Western journalists were kicked out of the region. Defence Secretary George Robertson said that strikes would continue 'for as long as it takes'. Critics in Britain and the United States warned that it could turn into a European Vietnam. Hundreds of thousands of ethnic Albanians fled Kosovo. The Serbs shot down a stealth bomber but the pilot escaped. They then captured three American soldiers on the Macedonian border, paraded them on TV and launched a show trial. The Allies stepped up their bombardment to include Milošević's administration and command centres in Belgrade.

'Maybe if I snorted coke and had one hot record I would be invited.' – Broadcaster David Dimbleby on not being asked to a 'Cool Britannia' Downing Street party.

April
The Northern Ireland peace talks were adjourned for ten days on the eve of Good Friday. The IRA revealed the location of the bodies of nine missing terrorist victims. Mo Mowlam threatened to impose proportional representation on the new Assembly if

the talks remained log-jammed over decommissioning. Later in the month negotiations resumed in Downing Street with Irish premier Bertie Ahern but remained deadlocked over para-military arsenals.

Macedonia expelled 30,000 Kosovan refugees in a midnight swoop. On the other side of the border 60,000 refugees were herded back to Priština, Kosovo's capital, as human shields. The NATO blitz was intensified when the aircraft-carrier *Invincible* was deployed. A further 1,800 British troops were sent to the Kosovo border, bringing the total to 6,000. Seventy ethnic Albanians were reported killed in an attack on their convoy by NATO planes. The air strikes continued night after night. Aerial photographs pin-pointed mass graves. NATO admitted that it might have misjudged the effect of an air war without ground troops ready to invade.

Two Libyans accused of the Lockerbie airliner bombing – Abdelbaset Ali Mohmed al-Megrahi and Al-Amin Khalifah Fhimah – were remanded in custody by a special Scottish court sitting in a Dutch army base.

The election campaign for the new Scottish Parliament opened. The SNP's poll rating slumped after it proposed a penny on income tax and after leader Alex Salmond condemned the bombing of Belgrade. Sean Connery later spoke at an SNP rally but failed to stir voters.

Jack Straw ruled that General Pinochet should face Spain's extradition proceedings.

William Hague's image was revamped as 'Bill Bloke'.

In London, a nail bomb exploded in Brixton, home to much of the capital's black population, injuring forty-eight. A week later another went off near Brick Lane, heart of the Asian community. It was followed the following month by a third in a Soho gay pub, which killed two and injured more than sixty. The bomber, neo-Nazi David Copeland, was eventually caught and sentenced to life.

May
Broadcaster Jill Dando was shot dead on the doorstep of her London home.

Tony Blair flew to Washington for NATO talks. He and Robin Cook signalled that ground troops could go in before a peace deal was agreed. The Serbian TV centre was hit as air strikes continued. Blair then visited Kosovan refugees just inside Macedonia. Cherie wept. Straw gave permission for 1,000 temporary refugees a week to enter the UK. A NATO strike hit the Chinese embassy in Belgrade, killing two and sparking the biggest diplomatic crisis of the war. Another fifteen civilians were killed by a rogue bomb which hit a market and a hospital; NATO claimed the casualties were being used as human shields. And eighty-seven members of a refugee convoy were killed by NATO bombs in an apparent blunder, in which the convoy was wrongly targeted.

Scotland, Wales and England went to the polls for devolution and council elections. Labour failed to win an outright majority in the Scottish Parliament (Lab 56, SNP 35, Con 18, LD 17, others 3). A similar failure for Labour occurred in the Welsh Assembly, where it won twenty-eight seats out of sixty. The Tories clawed back 1,200 English council seats. Low turn-outs were a feature of all polls. Donald Dewar was sworn in as Scotland's First Minister. John Reid succeeded him as Scottish Secretary, beating Helen Liddell, who replaced him as Transport Secretary. The Queen opened the new Welsh Assembly in Cardiff – the Manic Street Preachers refused to perform in the presence of royalty, but Tom Jones and Shirley Bassey had no such qualms.

Sixty-seven Labour MPs rebelled against a Bill to means-test incapacity benefits.

Jack Straw published a draft Freedom of Information Bill which had twenty-one escape clauses for public bodies trying to keep secrets.

Would-be BBC director general Greg Dyke gave £50,000 to Labour, it was revealed, and helped to finance the private offices of Tony Blair, Jack Cunningham and Mo Mowlam.

June
Prince Charles clashed with No. 10 by condemning genetically modified (GM) foods.

Slobodan Milošević surrendered to NATO terms, brokered by Finland and backed by the Russians. The deal involved rapid and verifiable withdrawal of all Serbian military, police and para-militaries from Kosovo; the deployment of UN security forces alongside NATO troops; the return home of a million Kosovan refugees; and a buffer zone between hostile forces. The bombing continued until there was firm evidence that Milošević was not bluffing. Days of wrangles followed but Serbian forces began to withdraw. British paratroopers and Gurkhas moved into Kosovo, but so did Russian forces, who had rushed through Serbia. The Russians reached Priština first and took the airport, ensuring an uneasy stand-off. Bill Clinton and Boris Yeltsin held talks to sort out the Russian role in the peace-keeping force. British troops uncovered evidence of mass murder, rape and torture by the Serbians.

A Sunderland ward scored the lowest-ever turnout – 1.5 per cent – in the European Parliament elections. Across the UK, barely one in four bothered to vote. The Tories emerged as the clear winners with thirty-four MEPs to Labour's twenty-six, the Liberal Democrats' nine and UKIP's three.

The government launched a campaign to reverse the increase in teenage pregnancies.

William Hague reshuffled his shadow Cabinet. Peter Lilley was sacked as deputy leader and Ann Widdecombe took the Home Office brief.

Screaming Lord Sutch hanged himself after thirty-six years as leader of the Monster Raving Loony Party.

The writer Paul Routledge said: 'People keep asking me if I was going to do a biography of Tony Blair but I wanted to write about a serious politician.' Tony Benn announced that he would be quitting Parliament at the next election to concentrate on 'serious politics'.

Jack Straw was forced to apologise after Passport Office delays led to long queues and missed holidays.

July

The Northern Ireland peace talks passed a crucial deadline at midnight on 30 June with no agreement. Sinn Fein ruled out an arms handover before joining a power-sharing executive; the unionists said: 'No guns, no government.' Blair urged the unionists to form an executive with Sinn Fein by 15 July, hinting that prisoner releases would be halted if the IRA did not disarm by May 2000. However, the process collapsed when the unionists rejected the plan.

The state opening of the new Scottish Parliament took place. The Queen was not invited to the party afterwards. The Scottish Office and the Scottish Executive blamed each other for the snub.

Stephen Byers unveiled a plan to partially privatise the Post Office. Blair pledged a ban on fox-hunting. The government lifted the ban on beef exports. Ministers confirmed that 51 per cent of air traffic control would be privatised. John Prescott hit out at 'faceless wonders' in No. 10 for undermining his transport strategy.

Tory party treasurer Michael Ashcroft was the subject of leaked

Foreign Office documents suggesting unconventional business practices abroad. He took legal action to dispute the claims.

Blair's summer reshuffle left the Cabinet unchanged except for the appointment of Paul Murphy as Welsh Secretary. Former coach Kate Hoey became Britain's first-ever female sports minister. Glenda Jackson left the ministerial bench to stand for London mayor. Tony Banks left to mastermind Britain's bid for the 2006 World Cup.

August

George Robertson was appointed secretary general of NATO.

The Blairs, on a free holiday in a villa at San Rossore, Tuscany, were branded 'scroungers' by local papers. Tony asked the Italian government to reopen a beach closed to give them privacy and promised to give an unnamed charity the cash he saved from the villa's rent. *Il Giornale*, an Italian national paper, ridiculed the couple's dress sense, comparing the Blairs to a railway worker and a waiter.

Charles Kennedy narrowly won the ballot for the Liberal Democrat leadership after four rounds.

Jack Straw was reported to the Commission for Racial Equality after he branded travellers as thieves.

John Prescott announced a public inquiry into the *Marchioness* riverboat disaster, almost exactly ten years after fifty-one party-goers died in the Thames.

North-western Turkey suffered a disastrous earthquake. Some estimates put the number of dead at more than 45,000; official figures gave the toll as a little over 17,000.

Hereditary peers, competing for a reprieve from instant abolition, were each given seventy-five words to justify their continued presence in the Lords.

September

Robin Cook again came under fire for continuing Hawk fighter jet sales to Indonesia, aircraft used to intimidate the East Timor independence vote. The people of that province nevertheless voted overwhelmingly for independence. Indonesian militia responded by slaughtering civilians as the army looked on. Around 1,000 people took refuge in the UN compound. Cook initially refused to block Hawk exports but was overruled by Tony Blair. Stephen Byers also halted the sale of British military vehicles to the regime. The UN Security Council agreed to send a peace-keeping force to East Timor, which would use 'all necessary measures' to restore order.

Mo Mowlam ruled that the IRA ceasefire remained intact despite some 'breaches'. Unionists threatened to boycott a review of the Good Friday peace agreement by George Mitchell, US special envoy to Northern Ireland. Mowlam said: 'You can't switch on peace like a light.'

Local activists rebuked Tyneside MPs David Clark and Steve Hepburn for being 'too Blairite'.

Former minister, diarist and self-confessed roué Alan Clark died. Michael Portillo, standing to replace him in the subsequent Kensington & Chelsea by-election, confessed to homosexual experiences during his Cambridge University days. Peter Lilley, helpfully, said: 'Homosexuality to me is as unappetising as eating cardboard.'

Great-grandmother Melita Norwood, 87, was exposed as a Soviet nuclear spy. Other alleged KGB moles were also outed.

Inflation hit a 36-year low.

Labour minister Ian McCartney's son died of a heroin overdose in a Glasgow bedsit.

Charles Kennedy told the Lib Dem conference that they would never become Labour's 'poodles'. He made Simon Hughes home affairs spokesman despite Hughes's attack on his own leadership.

The SNP's Annabelle Ewing cut Labour's majority in the Hamilton North by-election from almost 16,000 to under 600. Labour also held Wigan, but with support cut by two-thirds.

Blair told the Labour conference that the 'class war is over' but attacked the 'forces of conservatism'.

October

More than thirty were killed in the Paddington rail disaster. The government launched an immediate inquiry and signalled that

Railtrack was to be stripped of responsibility for rail safety.

Lady Thatcher's presence at the Tory conference stole William Hague's thunder. Hague called Tony Blair a fraud.

Peter Mandelson returned to the Cabinet as Northern Ireland Secretary, just ten months after he quit in disgrace. Mo Mowlam was demoted to Cabinet enforcer in the reshuffle, replacing Jack Cunningham. Frank Dobson resigned to stand as London mayor and Alan Milburn became Health Secretary. His first move was to pledge an extra £50 million to fight heart disease.

The Tories showed every sign of disintegration. Hague's Eurosceptic stance was attacked by John Major, Chris Patten and Lord Hurd, while Michael Heseltine and Ken Clarke shared a platform with Blair and Charles Kennedy at the launch of the Britain in Europe campaign. Right-wingers accused them of treachery. Launching a Scottish campaign to save the pound, Malcolm Rifkind said: 'The single currency is not just for Christmas . . . it's for ever.'

The government suffered six defeats in three days as the Lords rejected curbs on entitlement to disability benefit. Labour peer Lord Ashley said: 'Making the poor disabled pay for the very poor disabled is simply unacceptable.'

The Earl of Burford, a descendant of Charles II's mistress Nell Gwynn, stood on the Woolsack in protest at the abolition of hereditaries.

A new storm over the continuing French ban on British beef erupted after it was revealed that French livestock was being fed raw sewage. Agriculture minister Nick Brown announced his own boycott of French foodstuffs but was slapped down by Blair, who described it as 'stupid'. EU scientists ruled that the French ban was illegal. Later Brown was accused of giving in to the French after he agreed to further safety checks on British beef.

November

Michael Portillo won the Tory nomination for Kensington & Chelsea, saying: 'You can't put a cigarette paper between me and William Hague.' Later in the month he won the by-election on a 29 per cent turnout.

Gordon Brown unveiled £1 million tax breaks on share options for bosses.

Fifty-four Labour MPs rebelled on incapacity benefits means-testing.

Seventy-five hereditary peers won an internal election to stay in a reformed House of Lords. Those who failed were given a glass of champagne. One said: 'It was fun while it lasted.'

Scottish Tory leader David McLetchie, whose wife died of cancer, called for cannabis to be legalised for medicinal purposes.

Brown's pre-Budget report gave free TV licences to the over-75s, scrapped fixed price rises for petrol and pledged that cigarette taxes would go direct to the NHS.

Hopes for peace in Northern Ireland rose after the IRA offered a clear commitment to ending violence, but Ulster Unionist leader David Trimble failed to win over a majority of his Assembly members because there was no clear timetable on decommissioning.

The Queen's Speech included a new anti-terrorist Bill to target animal rights and religious extremists, the removal of safety powers from Railtrack, a crackdown on runaway fathers, the lowering of the gay age of consent to sixteen (again, after the debates ran out of time the previous year), automatic drug-testing of suspects, the Freedom of Information Bill and a utilities Bill to increase the power of watchdogs to curb domestic fuel costs.

Labour's London mayoral selection descended into shambles, with Ken Livingstone allowed to go forward as Frank Dobson threatened to pull out. For the Tories, Lord Archer was forced to quit the London mayoral race after admitting he persuaded friend Ted Francis to give him a false alibi in a libel case twelve years earlier, for which he won a £500,000 pay-out. William Hague's previous endorsement that Archer was a man of 'probity and integrity' came back to haunt him. Hague responded: 'This is the end of politics for Jeffrey Archer. He has let the Conservative Party down badly.' Archer was stripped of the Tory whip. Gordon Brown joked: 'What do you call a Tory candidate whose name starts with A? The accused.'

It was revealed that Tory treasurer Michael Ashcroft donated more than £80,000 a month to the party from Belize, despite Hague's public veto on overseas handouts.

The Queen awarded the George Cross to the Royal Ulster Constabulary, which lost 302 officers in the Troubles. Sinn Fein dismissed it as a cynical bid to win over unionist doubters. The unionist ruling council voted 480 to 329 in favour of the peace deal allowing Sinn Fein to join the Northern Ireland Executive before the handover of IRA arms. They signalled, however, that the vote could be reversed if decommissioning did not start by February. David Trimble said: 'We've done our bit, Mr Adams, it's over to you. We've jumped, you follow.' Tony Blair said: 'We have the best prospect in a generation for replacing violence and terror with peace and democracy.' But the Reverend Ian Paisley said: 'Any unionist who backed Trimble was as much an enemy of Ulster as the IRA.'

December

At midnight on 1 December power was transferred to the new Northern Ireland Assembly. Former IRA commander Martin McGuinness joined the executive as education minister, saying 'Ta' when accepting the job. Ian Paisley's Democratic Unionists refused to sit with Sinn Fein. Peter Mandelson said that it was one instance when he was happy to do himself out of a job.

The government lifted the beef-on-the-bone ban. Britain took action through the EU against the French for their continued illegal ban on British beef imports. At a Helsinki summit Blair said he would not go around 'handbagging' anyone.

The Tory selection for London mayoral candidate matched Labour's for shambles. The blue-rinse brigade blocked Steven Norris, although the party leadership promptly reinstated him.

Blair said that the north–south divide was no longer clear cut, infuriating northern Labour MPs.

Neil Hamilton lost his libel action against Mohammed al-Fayed after a £2 million trial, saying: 'I feel cold inside.' Fayed said: 'Christmas has come early.'

Tory MP Shaun Woodward defected to Labour. The Tory civil war deepened as Kenneth Clarke told William Hague to halt the party's lurch to the right and John Major told him not to allow Lady Thatcher to lead him 'by the nose'. Lord Tebbit and Norman Lamont led the counter-attack.

Boris Yeltsin announced that he was quitting as Russian President.

2000

Fuel protests came close to crippling the nation as Blair prepared for another general election.

January

The millennium bug failed to materialise.

In the New Year Honours list Elizabeth Taylor, Shirley Bassey and Julie Andrews became dames, while Sean Connery and Richard Branson were knighted.

Cherie Blair was fined £10 for failing to buy a rail ticket to Luton, where she sat on the bench for the first time. She claimed that the automatic ticket machine would not take credit cards or escudos – she had just returned from holiday.

Cheltenham MP Nigel Jones was attacked in his constituency office by a man waving a samurai sword. His aide, Andrew Pennington, was killed. Assailant Robert Ashman later pleaded guilty to manslaughter.

Only 11,000 people visited the Millennium Dome each day

during the month, 3 per cent of the target for the whole year. Chief executive Bob Ayling later resigned.

A newspaper claimed that in 1992 Gordon Brown had bought his Westminster flat at a knock-down £130,000 from AGB Research, a company which had gone into liquidation and which had been part of the late Robert Maxwell's empire. Brown insisted there had been 'no impropriety in the deal'. He later sold the property for £350,000.

Scottish Executive member Philip Chalmers was arrested for being drunk while driving in a red-light district. He resigned the £50,000-a-year job.

February

An investigation at Alder Hey Children's Hospital in Liverpool found that 850 organs taken from dead children were being kept in pots in a laboratory.

Dr Harold Shipman was jailed for life for the murder of fifteen women patients. The investigation suggested he might have killed 192. Lord Laming was appointed head of an inquiry to look into safeguards against killer GPs.

Peter Mandelson suspended the Northern Ireland power-sharing executive after adjudicator General John de Chastelain reported no progress on IRA arms decommissioning, despite an eleventh-hour IRA offer to produce a timetable for the handover. President Clinton urged the opposing parties to 'belly up to the bar'.

Michael Portillo returned to the opposition front bench as shadow Chancellor and announced that a future Tory government would keep the minimum wage and Bank of England independence, both introduced by Labour. John Redwood was sacked as environment spokesman and replaced by Asda boss Archie Norman. Lord Archer was kicked out of the party for five years.

Welsh First Secretary Alun Michael resigned and was replaced by Rhodri Morgan, previously blocked by Tony Blair.

An Afghan airliner was hijacked and flew into Stansted. The passenger hostages were freed after a three-day stand-off, many then seeking asylum in Britain.

The government headed off a backbench revolt by agreeing to raise the minimum wage by 10p to £3.60 an hour and the youth rate by 20p to £3.20, as the Low Pay Commission had recommended. Unemployment hit its lowest total in twenty years, falling by 9,800 to 1.58 million. Gordon Brown announced 'hit squads' for unemployment blackspots, including Glasgow and north-east England, saying that shirkers would see their benefits axed. He claimed that vacancies at Jobcentres almost matched the jobless total.

Tory MP Michael Colvin and his wife died in a fire while sleeping in their mansion.

March
A report revealed that the British Army rifle jammed when hot.

Health worker Nicci Dorrington called Tony Blair a liar during the PM's speech on the NHS and, after fleeing No. 10 minders, said: 'I would have stayed to say more but I was afraid of being lynched.'

International Development Secretary Clare Short and Defence Secretary Geoff Hoon argued over delays in British supplies getting to flood-hit Mozambique.

The Blairs took out an injunction to stop the publication of memoirs by former nanny Ros Mark.

Ken Livingstone announced that he would stand as an independent candidate for London mayor. Frank Dobson said: 'The ego has landed.' Commons watchdogs condemned Livingstone for allegedly failing to declare £158,000 in outside earnings.

John Prescott approved plans for 215,000 new homes in southeast England.

Peter Mandelson was forced to apologise after calling the Household Cavalry 'chinless wonders' – many died in Northern Ireland.

Cherie Blair was dubbed a 'trophy wife' by her half-sister Lauren Booth.

Gordon Brown's Budget included £2 billion more for the NHS and £1 billion more for schools; 25p extra on cigarettes; an increase to £214 for working family tax credit, and to £150 for pensioners' winter fuel payments; and 2p on a litre of petrol.

David Trimble fended off a leadership challenge in his Ulster Unionist Party but won only 57 per cent of the vote.

An MI5 laptop was left in a London tapas bar by a drunken agent.

Charles Kennedy revealed that he had taken lessons in how to walk on and off a public platform.

'For a control freak, Mr Blair's not very good at it, is he?' – Aline Templeton of Perth, in a letter to the *Times*.

April

Thirty-three new working peers were appointed to the Lords. William Hague insisted that Michael Ashcroft should be one of them. Cynics said that his title should be Lord Ashcroft of Belize. Tony Blair's father-in-law, actor Tony Booth, said: 'It would seem that the purpose and role of the House of Lords is redefined only in that it is now to be stuffed with Tony's cronies and William's bankers.'

Stephen Byers was grilled over his role in BMW's sale of Rover, a move which threatened 10,000 jobs.

Asylum-seekers faced a clampdown as a new Immigration Act came into force.

More than forty Labour MPs defied their whip and voted for uprating pensions in line with average earnings. Labour chiefs denied a report that they had dismissed the elderly as 'Conservative and often racist'.

Estimates of the cost of building the new Scottish Parliament at Holyrood spiralled from £40 million to £230 million. It was dubbed 'Donald's Folly' after First Minister Dewar.

Lord Archer was arrested and bailed after being questioned about an alleged conspiracy to pervert the course of justice. Conservative Central Office said: 'He's not a member of this party and it's nothing to do with us.'

Hague unveiled Tory plans to put asylum-seekers in secure prison camps. He also demanded that the law should be changed so that people could protect their homes after farmer Tony Martin was convicted of murdering a sixteen-year-old burglar.

On the second anniversary of the Good Friday agreement, Gerry Adams said that the peace process was at an all-time low.

The National Audit Office reported that British forces nearly ran out of ammunition during the Kosovo war.

'When a man's gotta go, he's gotta go.' – Michael Heseltine, announcing he was standing down at the next election.

'The trouble with power is that those who wield it never feel they have quite enough.' – Lord (Bill) Deedes.

May

Blair's Black Thursday: Labour lost almost 600 council seats, mainly to the Tories, in local elections. Ken Livingstone became London mayor with 39 per cent of the first-choice votes, beating Frank Dobson and Steven Norris.

Tony Blair went to Belfast to broker an apparent advance in the stalled peace process. The IRA issued a statement promising to put its arms 'completely and verifiably beyond use' and to open its arsenal to an international decommissioning body. Blair and Bertie Ahern prepared to reactivate the suspended Assembly. Later in the month David Trimble narrowly won a 459-403 vote in his party's ruling council to support the return to a power-sharing Assembly. Peter Mandelson hailed it as a breakthrough. President Clinton said: 'The wind is back in the sails of peace.'

Anti-capitalism demonstrations left the Cenotaph daubed in graffiti and Churchill's statue in Parliament Square sporting a grass Mohican haircut.

British troops began a refugee evacuation operation as Sierra Leone exploded into civil war.

Rover was bought by the Phoenix consortium for £10, with BMW promising to lend £500 million to help restructuring. Ford announced that its Dagenham plant was to shed 1,900 jobs.

Forty-six Labour MPs rebelled over the part-privatisation of air traffic control and their opposition was later strengthened when the system's computers crashed.

Jack Straw granted an entry visa to convicted rapist Mike Tyson for a Glasgow boxing bout.

Cherie Blair gave birth to son Leo, conceived while on holiday in Tuscany, at the age of forty-five. Tony Blair said of her: 'Once she goes to sleep it takes a minor nuclear explosion to wake her up.'

June

Blair suffered catcalls, slow handclaps and walk-outs when he addressed the Women's Institute at Wembley. He opened by saying: 'This is the most terrifying audience I have ever seen in my life.' No. 10 denied trawling websites for material to use against the protestors.

A leaked memo from No. 10 guru Philip Gould suggested that the government was seen as out of touch. Labour's opinion poll lead slumped to 3 per cent.

More than 500 England fans were deported from the Netherlands before and after the Euro 2000 defeat of Germany.

Fifty-five illegal Chinese immigrants were found suffocated to death in a container lorry at Dover, sparking a crackdown on 'snakehead' gangs and people-traffickers.

Independent weapons inspectors were shown their first IRA arms dumps.

Labour peer Lord Levy, Blair's Middle East troubleshooter, was alleged to have paid just £5,000 tax in a year despite his considerable fortune.

Blair proposed £100 on-the-spot fines for drunken hooligans.

July

Multi-millionaire author and Labour fund-raiser Ken Follett branded Blair 'unmanly' because of spin doctors briefing against ministers, including Mo Mowlam. He also labelled Mandelson 'Lady Macbeth'. In No. 10 Alastair Campbell reacted furiously, saying dismissively: 'Tony Blair is not a socialite.' Former welfare minister Frank Field threatened to expose the rubbishing of ministers during his term in office. Blair fumbled Prime Minister's Question Time, saying: 'Let's concentrate on spin, not substance.' BBC2's Michael Cockerell lifted the lid on Campbell's Downing Street operation.

Blair's sixteen-year-old son Euan was arrested for being drunk and incapable in Leicester Square after celebrating the end of his GCSEs. He was given a formal police warning and Blair said: 'He's basically a good kid.'

At Drumcree police used water cannon for the first time in thirty years anywhere in the UK to enforce a ban on the annual Orange march. Milltown Cemetery killer Michael Stone and almost ninety other convicted terrorists were released early under the terms of the peace process, emptying the Maze prison.

The government's gimmicky annual report was branded 'Pulped Fiction'.

The Blair Decade

Gordon Brown's comprehensive spending review promised an extra £43 billion over three years, including £13 billion for health and £12 billion for education.

The government was rocked by another leaked memo from polling guru Philip Gould, which warned that New Labour was seen to be not delivering and lacking patriotism.

Jack Straw was a passenger in a car caught doing 103mph on a motorway.

A Concorde crashed near Paris, killing 114.

Betty Boothroyd stood down as Madam Speaker, saying: 'Time's up.'

The Millennium Dome was to be sold to Nomura, a Japanese bank, it was announced. The bank later pulled out of the deal.

A row erupted over photographs taken at Leo Blair's christening and the normal family holiday photo-call was cancelled, although the Blairs later relented.

John Prescott came under fire for a £13,000 carpet in his refurbished grace-and-favour flat.

'Politics was a waste of time.' – Former Tory premier Ted Heath.

August

Gordon Brown married Sarah Macaulay at his North Queensferry home.

A leaked Tory document judged the party to be out of touch on sex and marriage. William Hague boasted that he drank 14 pints of beer a day when a teenager.

Madonna spurned a UK hospital for the birth of her baby, saying they were 'Victorian'.

A week of infighting between rival loyalist paramilitaries left three dead. Peter Mandelson revoked the parole of Johnny 'Mad Dog' Adair.

Comic Jim Davidson replaced Lord Archer as principal Tory fund-raiser.

Julia Langdon's biography of Mo Mowlam claimed that Mandelson and Charles Powell, the PM's chief of staff, conspired against Mowlam and Frank Dobson. The book also said that she complained that Blair treated her like a tea lady during President Clinton's visit to Belfast.

September

Mo Mowlam announced that she was to quit as both MP and minister at the next election, but denied she was being squeezed out. More books claimed feuds involving Tony Blair, Gordon Brown, Peter Mandelson and Mowlam.

Picketing at the Shell refinery at Stanlow, Cheshire, protesting against fuel duty levels, grew into a UK-wide demonstration, sparking panic buying. The government was taken completely by surprise. Petrol pumps ran dry, supermarkets briefly imposed food rationing and the Army was put on standby as the Privy Council approved emergency powers. After seven days of national crisis, the pickets called it off, claiming a moral victory and huge public support. They gave Gordon Brown thirty days to cut fuel duty.

The Liberal Democrat conference backed gay marriages.

The Labour conference voted by a 60-40 margin for an immediate and substantial rise in the basic state pension and a future link to average earnings. Blair said: 'I am listening. I hear. I will act.' The PM's keynote speech ended with his shirt drenched in sweat. Former minister Peter Kilfoyle warned that neglect of the Labour heartlands could push some voters towards extremism. Mowlam asked for a pat on the back because 'I'm about to burp'. Baby Leo was told he needed a picture for his conference pass.

Charlie Whelan, Gordon Brown's former spin doctor, said that Mandelson was turning a few heads with a new hairdo tinted 'Brazilian plum'.

'I never liked it . . . it's been a flop.' – Clare Short on the Dome.

October
At the Tory conference sixteen-year-old Ruth Evans asked

William Hague if he would send his children to state schools. Ken Clarke branded Michael Portillo's euro stance as 'blithering economic nonsense'. Hague challenged Tony Blair to a snap election and proposed regeneration companies for inner cities, 'cops in shops' and the demolition of 1960s and 1970s tower blocks. A third of the shadow Cabinet admitted they smoked cannabis during their youth.

Slobodan Milošević was toppled in a near-bloodless one-day revolution. He was replaced as Yugoslav President by Vojislav Koštunica.

Scottish First Minister Donald Dewar died after a fall outside his home.

A stolen Second World War Enigma decoding machine was sent to broadcaster Jeremy Paxman by post.

Four people were killed and thirty-four injured when a high-speed train was derailed near Hatfield, Hertfordshire. The Tories admitted they had blundered over the way British Rail was privatised. Railtrack closed the west coast main line, and safety checks and speed restrictions caused chaos across the network for months.

Michael J. Martin, a former apprentice sheet metal worker, was elected Speaker of the House of Commons. Parliamentary standards watchdog Elizabeth Filkin investigated claims that odds on Martin with bookies William Hill had gone from 20-1 to 8-11 as a result of several large bets. She found that Frank Roy MP, aide to John Reid, had made one of the bets. He said: 'If the bookies are daft enough to offer odds like that then they deserve to lose money.'

Lord Justice Woolf set an eight-year tariff on the killers of toddler James Bulger.

Lord Phillips published a devastating report into the CJD outbreak, blaming a string of former Tory ministers and civil servants for failing to alert the public to the danger. Blair pledged to set up a care fund for the families affected.

November
In a mini-Budget Gordon Brown cut fuel duty on 'green' fuel by 2p a litre and reduced the cost of road tax for less polluting vehicles. A 'Jarrow Crusade' by fuel protestors flopped.

A National Audit Office report condemned spending on the Dome. Leaked Cabinet papers showed that most senior ministers opposed the project but dared not go against Blair. Maverick Labour MP Bob Marshall-Andrews said: 'This confirms what we suspected all along. This whole disaster did not reflect the will of an incoming Labour government, but the vanities of a much smaller group who were seeking a totem pole for their own brand of instant populist policies.'

Paddy Ashdown's former mistress, Tricia Howard, claimed that he once had sex in nine and a half seconds.

Alastair Campbell attended a Britney Spears concert and the subsequent party.

George W. Bush won the US presidential elections, beating Democrat Al Gore, amid claims of vote-rigging. The result hung on the key state of Florida, where Bush's overall majority was just 537 votes. It was only the fourth time in America's history that the race was won without a plurality, the previous elections being 1824, 1876 and 1888.

Tony Blair agreed to commit British troops to a European rapid reaction force.

John Prescott stormed out of a global warming summit, accusing French environment minister Dominique Veynet of weakness. She called him 'macho'.

In Peckham, south London, ten-year-old Damilola Taylor was stabbed to death in the stairwell of a block of flats. The tragedy shocked the nation.

December
The Queen's Speech included curfews for under-sixteens, £100 spot fines for drunken yobs, the registration of bouncers, a ban on fox-hunting, the abolition of the right to a trial by jury and a crackdown on welfare cheats. William Hague said: 'There was so little in it that it was very good of Her Majesty to bother to come down and announce it.'

Peter Mandelson claimed that George W. Bush had 'green

Republican' sympathies. After thirty-six days of court hearings, Bush was finally confirmed as US President.

An EU summit in Nice became deadlocked when the French proposed that benefit payments and tax harmonisation should be subject to qualified majority voting. Blair claimed a victory after five all-day and all-night sessions.

2001

Crises over foot-and-mouth and Northern Ireland and a second general election victory were overshadowed by 9/11 and Blair's second major war.

January
Tony Blair was hit on the back by a tomato as he prepared for the general election campaign. William Hague launched a poster campaign on the theme of 'You've paid your tax, so where's your money gone?' An attempt to project the slogan onto the Millennium Dome was foiled by security guards.

Robert Bourne, a property developer, successfully bid for the Dome after, it was claimed, he gave Labour a £100,000 donation. Gambling tycoon Stuart Wheeler pledged £5 million to Tory funds, but said he would not give a penny if Ken Clarke became leader.

The Post Office was renamed Consignia.

Lady Justice Butler-Sloss ruled that the young killers of toddler James Bulger should be granted anonymity for life. The neglect, torture and murder of eight-year-old Victoria Climbié exposed the failings of the child protection system.

The cash-for-passports scandal forced Peter Mandelson to resign a second time. It was claimed that he misled colleagues over his role in passing on the passport application of tycoon Srichand Hinduja, a member of a family which later donated £1 million to the Dome. Alastair Campbell briefed that Mandelson was 'slightly detached' and questioned his emotional state. Cabinet colleagues Geoff Hoon and Stephen Byers also put the boot in. The night before Mandelson's resignation, Labour MP Peter Kilfoyle described him as 'Billy No-Mates'. Mandelson's former aide, Derek Draper, said: 'Peter has to learn to stay away from rich, glamorous people because he seems to go ga-ga when he has anything to do with them.' John Reid replaced him as Northern Ireland Secretary. An inquiry headed by Sir Peter Hammond subsequently cleared Mandelson, who then decided he should not have been forced out and hired lawyers. Europe minister Keith Vaz's own links to the Hindujas were exposed.

Liberal Democrat MEP Chris Davies demanded the legalisation of brothels.

The Redfern report into Alder Hey condemned former pathologist Dick van Velzen, who collected 2,000 children's hearts, 1,000 foetuses and the heads of youngsters aged from eight days to eleven years. Chief Medical Officer Liam Donaldson's separate report revealed that 104,000 body parts were then being held in hospitals across the country. Health Secretary Alan Milburn promised to make human tissue retention without family consent a criminal offence.

February

The Tories announced that they would target 'pebbledash' voters (houseproud suburbanites with their own car, many having bought their home from the council) in the forthcoming election. They promised tax concessions to parents who work at home, and cheaper private healthcare. Alan Milburn unveiled a £3 billion programme of hospital renovations.

The Commons Administration Committee agreed to a statue of Margaret Thatcher being erected in the members' lobby, facing Winston Churchill, Clement Attlee and David Lloyd George.

The United States and the UK launched air strikes against radar installations near Baghdad and outside Iraq's no-fly areas.

Lord Chancellor Lord Irvine urged lawyers, who look to him for promotion, to give generously to Labour. Tony Blair, in humble mood, admitted that the pace of change was too slow. He announced two weeks' paternity leave, instruction in the three Rs for illiterate benefit claimants and a register of hard drug-users. The business bible *Forbes* magazine dubbed Blair 'red tape Tony' for choking companies with bureaucracy.

Foot-and-mouth disease returned to Britain after twenty years. As it spread, beef exports were banned, thousands of carcasses burnt and travel restrictions put in place.

March

Ten people were killed and seventy injured in a rail crash near Selby, North Yorkshire, involving a passenger train, a freight train and a Land Rover.

A car bomb exploded outside the BBC in London and the splinter Real IRA were blamed.

Gordon Brown's Budget saw a freeze on petrol, booze and car taxes; maternity leave extended from eighteen to twenty-six weeks; increased tax credits for children and working families; more tax cuts for the low paid; £2 billion more for hospitals and schools; and a £49 billion repayment of the national debt. Unemployment fell below the million mark for the first time in almost twenty-six years. Election expectations soared.

Foot-and-mouth became a national crisis with more than 400 reported cases. Chief Veterinary Officer Jim Scudamore warned it could last six months. Scientific reports predicted 4,000 cases by July, which would result in half Britain's livestock being destroyed. The government ordered the slaughter of millions of healthy animals and farmers threatened an armed revolt. Tony Blair, at a Stockholm summit, let slip that he had ten days to decide the election kick-off.

John Prescott announced that the part-privatisation of air traffic control would involve a consortium of Richard Branson's Virgin Atlantic and British Airways. But talks over the partial sell-off of London Underground collapsed.

The Lords rejected both an outright ban on fox-hunting and also a compromise.

April

As foot-and-mouth continued to spread and the number of slaughtered carcasses approached one million, Blair postponed the local and general elections, originally scheduled for 3 May.

Ian Paisley's Democratic Unionists forced the recall of the Northern Ireland Assembly to challenge displays of Easter lilies, a symbol of republicanism, in the building.

Tony Blair announced that youngsters who promised to behave might be given free CDs and trainers.

The Tories were hit by a race row over MP John Townend's remarks about Britain becoming a 'mongrel' nation. William Hague refused to expel him. All party leaders had previously signed a Campaign for Racial Equality pledge not to play the race card during the election.

'I've never understood the attraction of royalty. They're all bonkers.' – Consumer affairs minister Kim Howells.

May

Massive police numbers swamped May Day anti-capitalist demonstrators, corralling many for several hours in London's Oxford Street.

Tony Blair 'came out' as a spectacles-wearer.

Nelson Mandela, speaking in Leeds, said: 'I thank the people of Liverpool for the honour of becoming a citizen of this country.'

John Reid, reflecting a new mood of optimism in Northern Ireland, said: 'The only problem flying into Belfast these days is getting a seat in business class.'

Blair announced the general election for 7 June to an audience of London schoolgirls. Alan Milburn found more cash for maternity services, acute hospitals and dental practices. Former Tory MP Shaun Woodward was parachuted into the safe Labour seat of St Helens South. Married to an heiress, he was dogged on the campaign trail by Tories dressed as butlers. Labour claimed that Portillo aide Oliver Letwin let slip Tory plans of £20 billion in tax cuts rather than the £8 billion in their manifesto.

Labour suffered a Wobbly Wednesday. Jack Straw was heckled by the Police Federation; Blair was harangued by Sharon Storer over the cancer treatment of her partner; most spectacularly, John Prescott responded to a thrown egg by punching the thrower, countryside protestor Craig Evans. Blair shrugged off the incident with a laugh, saying: 'John is John.' For the first time the election campaign came alive.

The Tories hit hard at the government's record on asylum-seekers and were condemned by Liberal Democrat leader Charles Kennedy as 'mad, bad and dangerous'. Former James Bond and *Avengers* actress Honor Blackman joined Kennedy on the campaign trail. The Tories scored with claims that Labour would abolish the national insurance ceiling, costing wage-earners on more than £29,900 over £800 a year. But claims of a secret Euro-tax, disguised as a hike in VAT, were quickly rebutted by Brussels.

Breast-enhanced model Jordan stood as an MP in Greater Manchester with the promise of free cosmetic surgery for all. Ann Widdecombe said: 'Mine are natural – I don't need any enhancement.'

Margaret Thatcher told a Tory rally that she would never sign up to the euro and referred to a film poster of *The Mummy Returns*. A Tory fan implored her to come back and lead them. 'Wouldn't that be lovely,' she replied.

Lord Archer went on trial for perjury and perverting the course of justice.

Racial riots erupted in Oldham.

June
Paddy Ashdown, Michael Heseltine and Norman Fowler were among twenty-four newly created peers.

'I'm bored to death.' – John Cleese on the election.

7th: general election
Labour almost matched its 1997 landslide with a majority of 167. The Lib Dems finished with fifty-two seats. The Tories made only one net gain. William Hague immediately quit as leader, saying: 'We must accept the verdict of the voters and listen to what they have said.'

Tony Blair reshuffled his Cabinet, demoting Robin Cook to Leader of the Commons and making Jack Straw Foreign Secretary. David Blunkett took over the Home Office, while John Prescott was made Cabinet enforcer and his massive Department of Environment, Transport and the Regions was broken up. Charles Clarke became the new party chairman. Other winners were Patricia Hewitt, Trade and Industry Secretary; Tessa Jowell, Culture Secretary; Estelle Morris, Education Secretary; Margaret Beckett, Environment Secretary; Hilary Armstrong, Chief Whip. Alistair Darling was moved to Work and Pensions, while Stephen Byers took Transport.

Michael Portillo was the first to declare that he would be standing for the Tory leadership, promising a softer, more caring and inclusive party. Ann Widdecombe excoriated his 'little band of back-biters' and pulled out of the race to spend more time with her mother. Right-wingers Iain Duncan Smith and David Davis put themselves forward. Ken Clarke kept the party guessing by going to Vietnam for a tobacco company. But by the end of the month he had signed up to the leadership contest in pugnacious, pro-European fashion.

*

Blair gave himself and his Cabinet a 41 per cent pay rise, taking his own salary to £163,418. Billionaire Sir John Paul Getty gave £5 million to the Tories.

The Queen's Speech unveiled more creeping privatisation, with business interests moving into classrooms and the NHS. Lords seats for all hereditary peers were to be abolished, the right to a jury trial limited and the double jeopardy rules scrapped.

Lord Cullen's report on the Paddington rail crash slammed Railtrack's 'lamentable failures' to act on warnings that signals were dangerous.

The Parole Board freed Robert Thompson and Jon Venables eight years after they murdered Jamie Bulger.

'He loses his temper on Friday and doesn't find it again until Sunday.' – An unnamed civil servant on John Prescott.

July

Labour backbenchers threatened to rebel over health checks for the disabled.

David Trimble resigned as Northern Ireland's First Minister in protest at the IRA's failure to decommission arms.

The Tory leadership contest turned to farce when David Davis and Michael Ancram tied in last place. Reruns saw Ancram knocked out by one vote and Davis later bowed out. Michael Portillo's chances were hurt by his liberal views on cannabis and gay rights, and by journalist Amanda Platell's election video diary. Ken Clarke topped the poll among MPs, with Iain Duncan Smith in second place and Portillo knocked out. He quit the shadow Cabinet, saying he would look for a job in media or the arts.

Further race riots hit Bradford and Home Secretary David Blunkett threatened to deploy water cannon.

Gordon Brown confirmed that his wife Sarah was expecting their first child in February.

Tony Blair and Bertie Ahern produced a take-it-or-leave-it blueprint for lasting peace in Northern Ireland, with some concessions to the nationalists. The initiative coincided with the funeral in north Belfast of eighteen-year-old Gavin Brent, a Protestant shot dead by the loyalist Red Hand Defenders, who thought they were opening fire on Catholic lads.

August
The Real IRA detonated a car bomb in an area of pubs and clubs in Ealing, west London, injuring eleven. The IRA announced 'historic' progress towards a deal on decommissioning arms. Unionists rejected it as a sham. A 24-hour suspension of the Good Friday agreement failed to break the deadlock.

It emerged that thirty-seven farmers had claimed compensation of £1 million or more each for stock lost in the foot-and-mouth slaughter, prompting a Commons watchdog inquiry and EU threats to withhold grants pending a fraud probe. Eventually the cost to the taxpayer topped £2.7 billion after 5.7 million animals were killed.

Neil and Christine Hamilton were arrested and quizzed by police over claims that they committed a serious sexual assault on a woman, Nadine Milroy-Sloan, in an east London flat. They both vehemently denied the claims and launched a civil action against their accuser. Police quickly dropped the investigation against the Hamiltons and turned their focus onto Milroy-Sloan.

Record A-level and GCSE passes were achieved, prompting claims that the exams were getting easier.

The Blairs booked cheap holiday flights with Ryanair.

The Tory leadership contest turned into a civil war. Lady Thatcher waded in: 'I simply do not understand how Ken [Clarke] could lead today's Conservative Party to anything other than disaster.' John Major accused her of treachery in encouraging Euro-rebels to undermine his previous adminis- tration. Michael Heseltine warned that a Duncan Smith victory risked keeping Tories out of power for another fifteen years. Duncan Smith aide Edgar Griffin, a party member for fifty-three years, was expelled after his close links with the British National Party were confirmed. Outraged, he claimed that the manifestos of the two parties were virtually the same. Duncan Smith won the contest.

British troops were sent to Macedonia as part of a UN bid to disarm ethnic Albanian rebels. Sapper Iain Collins became the first British fatality when a rock was dropped on his Land Rover.

September
Catholic primary schoolchildren were terrorised by a mob and targeted by a pipe-bomber as they daily walked the gauntlet

outside the Holy Cross school in the Ardoyne area of Belfast. John Reid cut short his holiday to handle the crisis.

11th: Two hijacked airliners slammed into the World Trade Center in New York, collapsing its twin towers. A third flew into the Pentagon, and a fourth dived into a field, apparently after passengers fought back. The hijackers were armed only with penknives and box-cutters. The total death toll approached 3,000.

George W. Bush and Tony Blair declared war on global terrorism. Bush said: 'They were acts of war . . . This battle will take time and resolve, but make no mistake about it: we will win.' Blair co-ordinated a coalition of European nations before crossing the Atlantic in a whirlwind tour. Osama bin Laden, a Saudi billionaire and founder of the al-Qaida terrorist network, who was believed to be in Afghanistan, was named as the prime suspect but the Taliban regime refused to hand him over. Joint forces gathered for a huge military response. The UK government produced a dossier pointing to bin Laden and al-Qaida. Blair told a recalled Commons: 'They [the attacks] bear all the hallmarks of a bin Laden operation: meticulous planning, mass casualties, total disregard for civilian lives, multiple simultaneous attacks and the use of suicide attackers.' Blair later told the Labour conference: 'We do not act against Islam. True followers of Islam are our brothers and sisters in this struggle.' John Reid said that terrorism comes in many forms, not just an Arab in a desert waving a Koran. The Taliban leader, Mullah Mohammad Omar, said: 'The Americans do not have the courage to come here.'

*

Stephen Byers pulled the plug on Railtrack, putting the shambolic network under public administration.

October
Tony Blair travelled 5,000 miles in two days, visiting Russia, Pakistan and India, to keep the anti-terror coalition intact. Iran's neutrality was secured by Jack Straw during a visit to Tehran.

The Allied air offensive against Afghanistan began on the 7th. In nightly cruise missile and bombing raids, Taliban military bases, bin Laden training camps, airfields and missile sites were reported hit. Journalist Yvonne Ridley, a Territorial Army major, was released after being held by the Taliban for ten days. She later converted to Islam. Osama bin Laden warned that no Americans or Britons would be safe from further terror attacks. Blair visited Oman, Switzerland and Egypt.

Later, armed forces minister Adam Ingram announced that 200 Royal Marine commandos were being deployed in the war zone, with 400 more on 24-hour standby, a figure which later rose to 6,000. The bombardment of Afghanistan continued. The United States admitted several mistakes, including the bombing of a civilian area and a stray missile hitting forces of the anti-Taliban Northern Alliance. Admiral Sir Michael Boyce, the Chief of the Defence Staff, warned that the war could last several years. UK polls showed a majority of the public were in favour of a pause in the bombing. Blair flew to Wales, Syria, Saudi Arabia, Jordan, Israel, Gaza and Italy in forty-eight hours to maintain the coalition. He was publicly roughed up by Syria's President Bashar al-Assad.

Iain Duncan Smith failed to make a splash at a truncated Tory conference. One commentator said that he and William Hague on a platform together looked like 'Dolly Parton's cleavage'.

Jo Moore, special advisor to Stephen Byers, was reprimanded after it emerged she sent an e-mail to colleagues within an hour of the 9/11 attacks saying it was 'a good day to get out anything we want to bury'. Byers and Blair refused to sack her, even though Blair said her words were 'horrible, stupid and wrong'.

Units of US Special Forces and Britain's SAS moved into Afghanistan. Two Americans died in a helicopter crash, and twenty-five Taliban were reported killed in a night attack by US Army special forces. Labour backbencher Paul Marsden revealed details of an angry clash with chief whip Hilary Armstrong over his anti-war stance. He claimed he was also bullied, threatened and shoved around by more junior whips and their henchmen.

The Commons was suspended for an hour after a suspect package was found in the post room. A wave of anthrax alerts swept Britain. Blair decided to backdate legislation imposing seven-year sentences on hoaxers.

David Blunkett announced that cannabis was to be downgraded from Class B to Class C and that simple possession would no longer be an arrestable offence, while increasing penalties for dealers.

In another Northern Ireland breakthrough, General John de Chastelain confirmed that the IRA had decommissioned a 'significant' part of its arms stockpile. David Trimble led his ministerial team back into the devolved government. Four army listening posts were publicly dismantled. Blair said: 'We are a long way from finishing our journey but a very significant milestone has been passed.'

November
The first 6,800kg 'daisy-cutter' bomb was dropped on Taliban positions.

The Northern Ireland peace process was again thrown into crisis as David Trimble narrowly failed to get re-elected as First Minister when two of his own party members voted against him. He was saved when Alliance Party members redesignated themselves as unionists on a temporary basis. The Royal Ulster Constabulary was renamed the Police Service of Northern Ireland.

Tony Blair's 'doorkeeper', Anji Hunter, quit No. 10 for a £160,000 PR job with BP.

In Afghanistan, the Northern Alliance took the strategic city of Mazar-i-Sharif after American bombers pulverised Taliban positions. Herat fell next. After six weeks of bombing the Taliban forces fled Kabul without a shot. Osama bin Laden's deputy was killed in one air attack. The Taliban appeared to collapse after nine days of tough fighting in some areas, retreat in others. For the first time in years pop music was broadcast on Afghan radio and barbers reported a roaring trade in shaving off beards.

David Blunkett prepared a state of emergency Bill, with a return to internment without trial for those suspected of being terrorist masterminds. He hit out at 'airy-fairy' civil liberties protestors. The legislation was passed comfortably despite a rebellion by twenty-one Labour MPs.

Henry McLeish resigned as Scottish First Minister following claims that he did not declare rent earned from sub-letting his constituency office. Education Minister Jack McConnell emerged as the only candidate to replace him. He revealed that seven years before he had had an affair with Labour Party worker Maureen Smith.

Mo Mowlam condemned Blair's presidential style and sparked stories of a Blair–Brown rift. Gordon described Tony as 'the best friend I've had in politics'.

Western aid workers held in Afghanistan were released by Special Forces. The Taliban prepared for a last stand in Kandahar, although they proved to be a spent force in that city. Bin Laden was reported to be cornered in a 30-square-mile pocket close to the Pakistan border. Several hundred Taliban prisoners rebelled while being kept in a mud fort and all but eighty-three were slaughtered. Hundreds more Taliban surrendered or switched sides at Kunduz but foreign fighters linked to al-Qaida promised war to the death. The Northern Alliance agreed, reluctantly, to attend a conference in Bonn to discuss the future broad-based governance of Afghanistan.

Brown's pre-Budget report included the abolition of football pools tax, an extra £30 billion for the NHS and more generous annual state pension increases.

'Don't tell Tony I said that.' – John Reid after addressing attendees at a Belfast meeting as 'comrades'.

December

Tony Blair lifted the lid on the security forces and sent a letter of thanks to spymasters for the work of their 'unsung heroes'.

Westminster sleaze-buster Elizabeth Filkin resigned and, in a ferocious letter to the Speaker, claimed she was put under intense pressure by ministers and spin doctors not to do her job vigorously.

Northern Ireland police ombudsman Nuala O'Loan rejected pressure to water down or delay a report which claimed that two warnings had been given days before the Omagh bombing. Police chief Sir Ronnie Flanagan angrily denied allegations of a police and Special Branch blunder.

The Taliban surrendered their last stronghold in Kandahar and reported that Mullah Omar had been captured. Three Americans were killed by friendly fire. Tribesmen and the SAS besieged Osama bin Laden's cave complex at Tora Bora. The non-Taliban Afghan factions agreed a deal which would include two women in the new administration.

British primary children came near the top of international league tables for literacy, maths and science.

David Blunkett unveiled police reforms, including the recruit-ment of foreign officers. Much to his fury, fines on lorry-drivers found to have carried illegal immigrants were deemed by judges to be themselves illegal. Blunkett, ahead of reports on the northern race riots, said that ethnic minorities should strive to be more British.

'They stiffen but they do not curtsey.' – The Queen, reportedly, on Cherie Blair's legs.

2002

The long road to war in Iraq plus Cheriegate at home.

January
Gordon and Sarah Brown's premature baby, Jennifer Jane, died after ten days of life.

Tony Blair flew to the sub-continent as tensions between India and Pakistan threatened to explode.

The rail network appeared close to collapse through industrial action. Europe minister Peter Hain said that the UK had the worst railways in Europe. A row erupted when it emerged that former BBC boss Lord Birt was Blair's chief strategic advisor for the railways. The Strategic Rail Authority's ten-year plan involved little extra money and few new ideas.

Rioting returned to the streets of north Belfast and security minister Jane Kennedy, witnessing the violence up close and incognito, had her Land Rover petrol-bombed and stoned. Sinn Fein's Gerry Adams, Martin McGuinness and two others took up their offices in the House of Commons. Adams's decision to display an Irish tricolour in his caused outrage.

Health Secretary Alan Milburn sparked a row by announcing plans to allow private firms to take over failing hospitals. Another erupted over the allegedly poor treatment of 94-year-old Rose Addis in a London hospital. Iain Duncan Smith claimed that a dog would have been treated better. No. 10 was accused of a smear, suggesting she was a racist who had refused treatment because she didn't want to deal with black or Asian nurses. It emerged she received regular visits from two ethnic minority social carers.

Blair refused to condemn the US treatment of alleged al-Qaida prisoners, including some Britons, who were being manacled, blindfolded and held in open cages measuring 6 feet by 8 in Camp X-Ray at Guantanamo Bay, the US military enclave in Cuba. UN human rights commissioner Mary Robinson insisted they were prisoners of war and should be treated as such.

Radio 2's Jimmy Young told Blair: 'You didn't get where you are today by answering questions, did you?'

Former Cabinet minister Lord Wakeham quit as chairman of the Press Complaints Commission because of his entanglement in the Enron crash, the world's biggest-ever bankruptcy.

Lord Chief Justice Lord Woolf ruled that all mobile phone thieves should go to prison.

February
The government was caught in a growing storm over the safety

of the MMR triple vaccine. Tony Blair hinted that Leo had had it. More parents switched to single jabs despite an outbreak of measles.

The Commons Standards and Privileges Committee recommended that Keith Vaz be suspended for a month for allegedly obstructing Elizabeth Filkin's inquiry into dealings with the Hinduja brothers.

Blair faced new sleaze allegations over a letter sent in support of Indian billionaire Lakshmi Mittal's bid to buy a Romanian steel plant after donating £125,000 to Labour.

Transport spin doctors Jo Moore and Martin Sixsmith were dumped after a feud concerning an alleged e-mail suggesting that the funeral of Princess Margaret was, again, a good day to bury bad news. Allegations that their boss, Stephen Byers, had lied over the sacking of Sixsmith were described by Blair as 'Garbagegate'. Byers was forced to make a semi-apology in a Commons statement. It was alleged that he survived because rebellious Labour backbenchers were promised a free vote on fox-hunting.

March

Blair signalled that he was ready to back a US strike on Iraq, following evidence that Saddam Hussein's regime had taken 1,000 trucks provided for humanitarian aid and converted them into mobile rocket-launchers.

The number of people on hospital waiting lists went back over the million mark.

Thousands of disaffected police besieged Westminster in protest at David Blunkett's reforms, particularly cuts in overtime pay.

Barbara Windsor, Carry On star and landlady of the Queen Vic in *EastEnders*, pulled pints for MPs at the reopening of Annie's Bar.

Lady Thatcher suffered a second stroke and was told by her doctors she must not make any more speeches or public appearances.

Iain Duncan Smith declared that the Tories would from now on be the party of the vulnerable.

MPs again voted overwhelmingly for a total ban on fox-hunting with dogs.

Culture Secretary Tessa Jowell announced plans to scrap many of Britain's legal curbs on gambling, raising the prospect of Las Vegas-style resorts, walk-in casinos and million-pound jackpots.

Consignia announced that up to 40,000 postal workers might lose their jobs and 3,000 urban post offices might close.

April
Parliament was recalled for one day following the death of the Queen Mother, aged 101. An estimated 200,000 queued for her lying in state in Westminster Hall.

Teaching unions threatened industrial action unless their

workload was cut. Education Secretary Estelle Morris described their demands for a 35-hour week, already granted in Scotland, as 'potty'.

British Airways announced plans to axe 5,800 jobs, bringing total losses to 13,000 since the previous summer.

Gordon Brown's sixth Budget included 1 per cent on all national insurance contributions to fund a £40 billion cash injection for the NHS over five years, plus boosts for bingo-players, families, pensioners and small businesses.

The Lords blocked David Blunkett's bill to extend Home Office control over the police. Blunkett reinforced a pledge to give courts greater powers to lock up persistent offenders aged between twelve and sixteen.

A Palestinian refugee camp at Jenin was bulldozed in a nineteen-day battle with Israeli forces. Palestinians claimed it was a matter of ethnic cleansing, but Israel insisted that only terrorists were targeted. A peace mission by US Secretary of State Colin Powell was ineffective. Suicide bombings increased. Yasser Arafat, holed up in his Ramallah HQ, refused to sign a ceasefire. International condemnation was aimed at Israel's Ariel Sharon.

The Cabinet was split over a plan, backed by Tony Blair, to strip the parents of young hooligans and persistent truants of child benefit. Alistair Darling signalled that ministers would support a backbench Bill to deny 'neighbours from hell' housing benefit.

Tory frontbencher Ann Winterton was sacked for telling an anti-Pakistani joke at a rugby club dinner.

Culture Secretary Tessa Jowell published a draft Bill loosening the rules on media ownership, opening the way for Rupert Murdoch to buy Channel 5.

Another Hertfordshire rail crash, this time at Potter's Bar, killed nine and left fifty injured.

May

Cherie Blair revealed that their kids call the PM Lionel. It was also revealed that she has a previously unknown half-sister by her father, Tony Booth.

Tony Blair again came under fire after Labour took a £100,000 donation from Richard Desmond, publisher of the *Daily* and *Sunday Express* and such magazines as *Asian Babes*, *Horny Housewives* and *Mega Boobs*. Blair said: 'If someone is fit and proper to own one of the major newspaper groups in the country, there's no reason why we shouldn't accept donations from them.' It emerged that Desmond's takeover of Express Newspapers had been cleared by Stephen Byers during his stint as Trade and Industry Secretary.

Byers faced a new Commons onslaught over the sacking of Martin Sixsmith. He resigned, saying that he had never lied, but accepting that he had become a 'liability'. John Prescott accused the Transport Select Committee of stabbing Byers in the back. Committee member Louise Ellman said that criticism had been aimed at Prescott, not Byers.

Byers was replaced as Transport Secretary by Alistair Darling, Andrew Smith replaced him at Work and Pensions, while Paul Boateng replaced Smith as Chief Secretary to the Treasury, becoming the first black Cabinet minister.

The government finally got rid of the Millennium Dome by giving it free to developers Meridian Delta in return for a share of future profits.

Jack Straw failed to cool threats between Pakistan and India over Kashmir as border clashes threatened to escalate to nuclear warfare.

June

The Queen's Golden Jubilee celebration included a pop concert at Buckingham Palace.

Labour was again rocked, this time by claims that Department of Transport spin doctor Dan Corry asked for a probe into the political loyalties of the Paddington train crash victims.

No. 10 dropped a press complaints action against newspapers which alleged that Tony Blair tried to 'muscle in' on the Queen Mother's lying in state. Black Rod Sir Michael Willcocks was identified as a source.

Mick Jagger and Bobby Robson were knighted in the Queen's

Birthday Honours. So too was curry king Gulam Noon, a Labour donor.

Cherie Blair was in hot water when, hours after a Palestinian suicide bomber killed fourteen, she said that such youngsters are without hope when they blow themselves up. She quickly apologised for forgetting to offer sympathy to the victims and their families.

Blair held the first of his regular open press conferences at No. 10. He signalled that he would stay on beyond the next general election, saying he would be judged by substance, not spin.

Education Secretary Estelle Morris said she wouldn't touch some comprehensive schools with a barge pole.

'I feel like a teenager. I'm not going to try drugs or anything – but I'm free.' – William Hague on no longer being Tory leader.

'Just about the only thing less popular than the euro is the Tory Party.' – Iain Duncan Smith's chief strategist, Dominic Cummings, on why the party should stay out of the 'no' referendum campaign.

July
Teetotal Tory Sir Teddy Taylor claimed that MPs are drinking too much.

The stock market plunged with the crash of WorldCom.

London mayor Ken Livingstone offered to take a lie detector test over claims that he assaulted a guest at a party.

A private tutor taught the Blair children at No. 10, it was revealed. Estelle Morris unveiled plans for successful school heads to become chief executives of failing schools.

A one-night stand between Stephen Byers and a Liverpool councillor was exposed.

Iain Duncan Smith said that the Conservative Party was viewed as 'nasty, extreme and strange'. He dumped David Davis as Tory chairman. Alan Duncan came out as the first openly gay Tory MP.

David Blunkett announced plans for a national ID card. He later produced more plans to curb the number of jury trials, scrap the double jeopardy rule in serious cases and allow judges to reveal previous convictions in trials.

Gordon Brown's comprehensive spending review pledged a £61 billion boost for public spending over three years, with the lion's share going to education.

Up to 750,000 local government workers staged a one-day strike over pay.

The IRA apologised for the deaths of 'non-combatants' in the 1972 Bloody Sunday bombings. After an upsurge in street violence in Belfast, Tony Blair and John Reid promised to toughen ceasefire conditions, a move which threatened to expel Sinn Fein from devolved government.

A report by Dame Janet Smith reckoned that Dr Harold Shipman certainly killed 215 patients and probably murdered 45 more, making him Britain's biggest-ever mass murderer.

Lord Irvine's son faced jail in the United States over a stalking charge.

Arthur Scargill retired as National Union of Mineworkers president but kept his lavish home and a £12,000 annual consultancy fee.

The High Court ruled that Customs seizures from cross-Channel 'booze cruisers' were illegal.

August

John Prescott suggested that council tenants might lose their right to buy, introduced under Margaret Thatcher. No they won't, said Downing Street.

Cherie Blair suffered a miscarriage.

President Bush moved closer to military action against Saddam Hussein. Tony Blair remained his staunchest ally despite a growing backbench revolt against a strike on Iraq. US Defence Secretary Donald Rumsfeld compared Washington's enthusiasm for an attack to Churchill's call for rearmament in the 1930s.

The bodies of Holly Wells and Jessica Chapman, both aged ten, were found. Their school caretaker, Ian Huntley, was committed to Broadmoor and his girlfriend, Maxine Carr, was charged with conspiracy to murder.

The Earth Summit in Johannesburg saw Zimbabwean President Robert Mugabe dub Blair an imperialist.

September

The new Criminal Records Bureau failed to meet its deadline for vetting teachers before the start of the new academic year, and the government was forced to allow schools to take on unvetted staff.

A Blair–Bush summit at Camp David agreed to push for a new UN mandate against Iraq for failing to comply with weapons inspections. The TUC heard Tony Blair's conference speech in silence. Blair agreed to recall Parliament for a one-day debate on Iraq. The first anniversary of 9/11 was marked by a service in St Paul's Cathedral featuring 3,000 white rose petals. Blair published a 'dossier of terror' which claimed that Saddam could launch chemical weapons within forty-five minutes and was close to developing a nuclear bomb. Fifty-six Labour MPs rebelled after the recall debate.

Estelle Morris ordered the re-marking of thousands of A-level examination scripts following the discovery that exam boards had downgraded pupils' results to combat 'grade inflation'. An inquiry by Mike Tomlinson, chief inspector of schools, cleared Morris, but the head of the Qualifications and Curriculum

Authority, Sir William Stubbs, resigned. Three boards were ordered to review 350,000 papers involving 100,000 teenagers. Later fewer than 2,000 results were upgraded.

An estimated 400,000 people joined a countryside rally in London.

Charles Kennedy told the Lib Dem conference that they had overtaken the Tories as the main party of opposition. He said the shadow Cabinet was less visible than Lord Lucan.

Former minister Edwina Currie revealed that she had had a four-year affair with John Major from 1984. David Mellor branded her a 'trollop'.

The Labour conference was dominated by the Currie affair and a show-stopping performance by Bill Clinton. Blair suffered a defeat of private funding for public service projects but he defiantly pledged no slowdown in the pace of reform. 'We are best when we are boldest,' he said.

Peter Mandelson complained that no-one invited him to parties any more.

October

Power-sharing in Northern Ireland was again on the verge of collapse. Police raided Sinn Fein offices after receiving evidence that the nationalists were collecting the names and addresses of prison and police officers. Ian Paisley's DUP pulled its ministers out of the executive. David Trimble threatened to do the same unless Blair expelled Sinn Fein within six days. Later that month the executive was suspended.

At the Tory conference Iain Duncan Smith said: 'Don't underestimate the determination of a quiet man.' Lord Tebbit caused mayhem on the fringes, sparking calls for his expulsion.

Tony Blair failed to persuade Russian President Vladimir Putin to back a war on Iraq during a Moscow summit. In Washington it became clear that George W. Bush was planning an invasion to topple Saddam, 'unfinished business' from the First Gulf War led by his father. Saddam appeared to offer UN weapons teams unrestricted access. After three weeks of negotiations the five permanent members of the UN Security Council could not agree on the terms of a new resolution. Bush threatened to go it alone if necessary. An Iraqi referendum backed Saddam by 11,445,638 votes to nil.

A car bomb outside a nightclub on the holiday island of Bali killed more than 200, thirty-three of them Britons. Al-Qaida were the main suspects. Blair insisted that both the war on terror and on Saddam were justified. 'It's not either/or,' he said.

Lord Archer published his prison diaries, breaching regulations which forbid writing such a diary for profit without permission . . . Hot water in stir.

Peers threw out moves to allow unmarried couples, including gay couples, to adopt.

Estelle Morris resigned, saying she was not up to the job of Education Secretary. She was replaced by Charles Clarke, who in turn was replaced as party chairman by John Reid. Reid's position as Northern Ireland Secretary was taken over by Paul Murphy, and Murphy's old job as Welsh Secretary was given to Peter Hain.

Culture minister Kim Howells described entries in the annual Turner art prize as 'conceptual bullshit'.

MPs voted to reform House of Commons hours, with some sessions starting late morning and finishing early evening.

The Commons Home Affairs Select Committee condemned Operation Care and other police 'trawls' looking for historic child abuse cases in care homes.

November
Iain Duncan Smith told his party: 'Unite or die,' after Ken Clarke, Michael Portillo and other prominent Tories defied him to support gay adoptions.

The Queen's Speech included a crackdown on anti-social behaviour, new rape laws, a green light for English regional devolution and the creation of foundation schools outside local authority control.

Firefighters walked out on a 48-hour strike over pay, the first for twenty-five years. Blair vowed not to give in to them. John Prescott refused to sign a deal between the unions and employers for a 16 per cent pay rise, saying he would not sign a blank cheque. That sparked an eight-day strike. Army-crewed 'green goddess' fire engines were taken out of mothballs. Fire union leader Andy Gilchrist vowed to topple New Labour.

The Cabinet was divided over student top-up fees.

Gordon Brown's pre-Budget report included more cash for pensioners but also revealed a £30 billion increase in borrowing.

The Lords ruled that the Home Secretary did not have the power to set minimum tariffs for convicted murderers, theoretically opening jail doors to more than 200 killers.

December
A second eight-day strike was dropped by firefighters to allow the dispute to go to arbitration.

Government plans to outlaw hare-coursing and stag-hunting but permit other forms of hunting with dogs in certain areas under licence managed to outrage both sides of the hunting debate.

Downing Street was accused of lying over Cherie Blair's purchase of two Bristol flats, in which she used convicted conman Peter Foster as a go-between. The 'Cheriegate' row rumbled on, not helped by an apparently botched cover-up. Cherie claimed she knew nothing of Foster's background, even though he was the boyfriend of her lifestyle guru and dresser, Carole Caplin. Cherie made a tear-stained apology on live TV but insisted she did nothing wrong. New claims suggested she intervened on Foster's behalf as he fought against extradition to Australia. Both Blairs were seriously damaged and her hopes of becoming a High Court judge suffered accordingly. Cherie said: 'The reality of my daily life is that I'm juggling a lot of balls in the air . . . and some of them get dropped.'

Charles Kennedy was the guest chairman of an episode of the satirical TV quiz *Have I Got News For You*.

Geoffrey Robinson was charged with refusing to give a breath test but denied having drugs in his car.

Charles Clarke, denying that he is a bruiser, said: 'The word implies thuggery, bullishness and bullying.'

Iraq released a 12,000-page dossier purporting to show that they had no weapons of mass destruction. Tony Blair and Jack Straw said it was full of holes. The PM told British troops to prepare for war.

'Vicious, violent and horrible.' – Mo Mowlam on her former Cabinet colleagues.

2003

Blair fought and appeared to win the Iraq war but the bloody aftermath and the death of a scientist weakened his grasp on power.

January

Tony Blair delivered his gloomiest New Year message yet, warning of the threats of a world economic slump, war with Iraq and global terrorism. He said: 'I cannot recall a time when Britain was confronted simultaneously by such a range of difficult and, in some cases, dangerous problems.' Blair's own priest, Father Timothy Russ, accused him of 'moral surrender' over the impending war on Iraq. The Pentagon doubled troops in the Gulf region and the British aircraft-carrier *Ark Royal* headed for the war zone. Foreign Secretary Jack Straw said that the chances of war were 60-40 against but he was immediately slapped down by Blair.

'There's an old saying that you speak to the engineer, not the sweat rag.' – Commons Speaker Michael J. Martin on Labour spin doctors. He also described them as an 'absolute nuisance'.

Home Secretary David Blunkett planned five-year prison

sentences for 'gun-toting' after two teenage girls were shot dead outside a Birmingham hairdresser's.

Former Labour Cabinet minister and Social Democrat leader Roy Jenkins died.

Detective Constable Stephen Oakes was killed and four other police officers stabbed during an anti-terror raid on a Manchester flat following the discovery of the lethal poison ricin in north London. Blair linked the domestic terrorism threat to the proposed Iraq war.

Anti-war feeling grew and Church of England bishops said that war was unjustified. Blair insisted that Saddam Hussein would be forced to disarm, regardless of a second UN resolution. More than 35,000 troops, a quarter of the British army, were mustered for deployment in the Gulf. Police raided the Finsbury Park mosque in north London. The Western coalition came apart when France's President Jacques Chirac said that weapons inspections in Iraq should continue for several more months. But President George W. Bush's State of the Union speech made war seemingly inevitable.

Education Secretary Charles Clarke ploughed ahead with his plan to charge students top-up tuition fees of up to £3,000 a year. He confirmed that some graduates would be left with debts of £21,000.

Firefighters returned to arbitration after a further 24-hour stoppage. Deputy premier John Prescott resumed powers, suspended forty-four years previously, to set the pay and conditions of firefighters and signalled he would use them to impose a settlement on the dispute.

February

The build-up to war continued, with Britain sending more warplanes to the Gulf. Downing Street issued a new report detailing Saddam Hussein's alleged terrorist links. The exercise backfired when it emerged that whole pages had been lifted from a PhD thesis by a 29-year-old Californian academic, Ibrahim al-Marishi. Veteran leftie Tony Benn flew to Baghdad and interviewed Saddam. Dismissing it as a stunt, Blair said: 'I don't think Jeremy Paxman or John Humphrys are in any great risk.'

MPs voted down all options for House of Lords reform, from outright abolition to appointees only.

Prescott announced plans for massive new housing expansion in south-east England and the clearance of derelict and abandoned properties in the north. David Davis, his Tory shadow, told him: 'Your plan is to bulldoze the north and concrete the south.'

Teachers received a 2.9 per cent pay increase but the Lord Chancellor, Lord Irvine, got 12.6 per cent, worth an extra £22,000 annually. First he accepted the pay hike but an outcry forced him to cut it to 2.5 per cent.

More than 450 soldiers with tanks and 1,000 police ringed Heathrow airport after intelligence reports suggested a planned al-Qaida missile attack. John Reid warned of a 9/11-style attack on Britain.

An ICM poll showed that less than 10 per cent backed a war against Iraq without UN approval. The USA admitted that its fighter pilots were routinely issued with amphetamines before missions. Labour backbencher Ronnie Campbell, whose 27-year-old Marine son was stationed alongside Americans in Kuwait, branded it 'criminal'. Weapons inspector Hans Blix reported that Saddam was co-operating more fully and that the UN team had started to destroy stockpiles of prohibited chemicals. His unexpectedly upbeat verdict fuelled anti-war protests.

At least a million people joined an anti-war mass rally in London, Britain's biggest-ever demonstration. Speakers included Mo Mowlam, Ken Livingstone, Tony Benn, Vanessa Redgrave, Tim Robbins, Bianca Jagger, former US presidential hopeful Jesse Jackson and playwright Harold Pinter, who described Blair as a 'hired Christian thug'. Blair said that he understood their feelings but insisted there was a 'moral case' for removing Saddam by force. Ridding Iraq of Saddam would be 'an act of humanity' and to delay would make the future 'more bloody'.

Congestion charges were levied on the streets of central London by Mayor Ken Livingstone.

David Blunkett lost a High Court battle over his bid to deny benefits to asylum-seekers.

The Tories fell into another bout of internal blood-letting, with

Iain Duncan Smith describing Michael Portillo and other alleged modernisers as a 'cancer'.

Blair met the Pope, who told him: 'The future of humanity should never be tied down by terrorism and the logic of war. Never, never, never.' Blair suffered the biggest backbench revolt inflicted on any PM for a century when 122 Labour MPs voted for an amendment that the case for military action against Saddam was 'not proven'. They were joined by the Liberal Democrats and some Tories, including Ken Clarke. Blair ignored them. Saddam began to dismantle illegal al-Samoud 2 missiles, a move which Blix said was 'significant'.

'Whatever my mother-in-law gives me.' – Blair on what he would like for his fiftieth birthday.

March
Former Welsh Secretary Ron Davies announced he was leaving politics for good after a newspaper reported a liaison with a stranger at a beauty spot off the M4. He claimed that he had been 'watching badgers'.

France, Germany and Russia threatened to veto military action against Iraq. Tony Blair demanded that Saddam be given until 17 March to disarm or face the certainty of war. More Labour MPs threatened to rebel if action was taken without a second UN resolution. President Bush's patience ran out and Blair signalled that a second UN mandate was unlikely to happen. Overseas Development Secretary Clare Short described Blair's rush to war as 'reckless' and threatened to quit, but didn't. Robin Cook,

Leader of the Commons and ex-Foreign Secretary, and junior ministers John Denham and Lord Hunt did resign as a matter of principle. Blair and Bush outlined a 'road map' for a two-state solution to the Palestine crisis, which appeased some potential Iraq rebels but failed to prevent another huge Commons revolt. The President and the PM met in the Azores to finalise war preparations with or without a second UN resolution.

The war began in the early hours of the 20th (GMT) with a surprise missile attack on Saddam's bunker, followed by a massive air attack on Baghdad. Coalition troops moved into southern Iraq, taking the key al-Faw peninsula and encircling Basra. The first British casualties were eight dead in a helicopter crash; six more Britons and four Americans were killed when two Sea Kings collided. Iraqi resistance was met in the port of Umm Qasr and oil wells across the region were torched. Desert Rats and other columns pushed towards Baghdad. ITN reporter Terry Lloyd and two crewmen were killed by American 'friendly fire' and a British Tornado was shot down by a US Patriot missile. Many Iraqis surrendered but pockets of resistance proved fiercer than expected. Baghdad was bombarded day and night and Saddam's presidential compounds were repeatedly hit. Four US soldiers captured in heavy fighting were paraded in front of Iraqi TV cameras.

The second week of the conflict saw coalition supply lines under attack from irregular units, tank and artillery battles, serious fighting around Basra and on the road to Baghdad, and dozens of civilians killed in the capital's marketplace by coalition bombard-ment. Saddam's Republican Guard fired on civilians attempting to flee Basra, while others were mown down by jittery American troops. Casualties mounted, from both enemy action and friendly fire. Bush mobilised another 120,000 troops, while his Defence Secretary, Donald Rumsfeld, was attacked by military chiefs for interfering in detailed operational planning. UK Defence Secretary Geoff Hoon said it was always going to be a 'difficult and dangerous' war.

April

US Special Forces rescued nineteen-year-old Private Jessica Lynch from an Iraqi hospital a week after she was captured and wounded. Later it was claimed that she was being released anyway and the operation was a stunt for TV. Air strikes hit a Baghdad maternity ward, killing three. US Marines crossed the 'red zone' surrounding Baghdad and took the capital's airport. Tanks raced into the city centre in a raid, reportedly killing 1,000 defenders.

John Reid was appointed Leader of the Commons following the resignation of Robin Cook, and Ian McCartney replaced Reid as party chairman.

The BBC's John Simpson was wounded in another 'friendly fire' bombing, which also killed eighteen Kurds and three Americans. A US tank shell hit a hotel used by foreign journalists, killing one, wounding others and damaging the propaganda effort. More broadcasting and media centres were hit, blacking out Iraqi TV. British troops took full control of Basra, while the Americans moved closer to the centre of Baghdad. Four bunker-busting bombs destroyed a restaurant where, according to intelligence, Saddam Hussein and his two sons were dining. At a Belfast summit Tony Blair and George W. Bush agreed that the UN would have a 'vital role' in the rebuilding of Iraq and that the interim government will be 'of Iraqis, for Iraqis'.

Iraqi resistance melted away in Baghdad, Basra and Mosul and the Kurds helped take northern Iraq. The conventional war was effectively over after twenty-three days. Iraqi information minister Mohammed Saeed al-Sahhaf – known as Comical Ali – and other high-profile figures disappeared from sight. A giant bronze statue of Saddam was toppled with the help of an American tank crew and stamped on by celebrating Iraqi civilians. Serious disorder and mass looting broke out in all the major cities. The USA put a bounty on the heads of Saddam, his sons and his senior ministers and aides.

The cost of the war began to be counted, although the figures were later hotly contested: 2,320 Iraqi soldiers killed, 9,000 prisoners of war taken, and civilian casualties estimated at 1,400 dead and 5,103 injured. Coalition losses were: 105 US killed, 399 injured, eleven missing, seven PoWs (released); thirty-one British military personnel killed and seventy-four injured; ten journalists killed in action and two missing. During the war 30,000 air sorties were flown and 750 cruise missiles fired. Ali Ismaeel Babbas, a twelve-year-old boy who lost his family and both arms in a Baghdad bombing, was flown to Kuwait for life-saving surgery.

Donald Rumsfeld said: 'Saddam Hussein is now taking his rightful place alongside Hitler, Stalin, Lenin and Ceauşescu in the pantheon of failed, brutal dictators.' Sporadic fighting continued but the main effort switched to humanitarian aid, restoring law and order, hunting Saddam and searching for the elusive weapons of mass destruction which were the reason for invasion. Blair revealed that he would have resigned if he had lost the Iraq war vote in the Commons, and Jack Straw said he would have gone with him.

Gordon Brown's seventh Budget put 8p on cigarettes, gave £100 more to pensioners and established £250 baby bonds.

A report by Metropolitan Police commissioner Sir John Stevens concluded that rogue Army and RUC officers had helped loyalist terrorists murder Catholics in Northern Ireland.

The SARS virus spread from China to Canada and Britain, sparking fears of a worldwide pandemic.

May

At the close of the local elections poll, Tory industry spokesman Crispin Blunt quit in protest over Iain Duncan Smith's leadership. The Conservatives gained more than 500 council seats, mainly from Labour, taking Coventry for the first time in twenty-five years. The BNP became the second party on Burnley council.

Blair said he would answer to his 'Maker' for lives lost in the Iraq war. No. 10 spin doctor Alastair Campbell, asked about the PM's religious beliefs, said: 'We don't do God.' Peter Mandelson said he loved tickling and teasing Campbell because 'he doesn't like it'.

Anti-war MP George Galloway was suspended from the Labour Party.

Sixty-six Labour MPs rebelled against foundation hospitals. Clare

Short was the only minister who missed a vote without giving a reason. John Prescott's Bill to allow him to impose a settlement on the firefighters was opposed by twenty-seven Labourites. Short quit the Cabinet and blasted Blair. Other ministers turned on her. Mandelson told female lobby journalists that Gordon Brown was walking all over Blair on the euro. Ministers turned on him. Another row rumbled on over Blair's refusal to hold a referendum on the new European constitution.

Blair turned fifty.

Blair angrily denied that he 'sexed up' a pre-war report on weapons of mass destruction in Iraq. He was kissed by a small boy during a brief visit to Basra.

June

John Reid claimed that 'rogue elements' in the security forces were spreading false information about the coalition's failure to find weapons of mass destruction in Iraq. Six military police officers were killed by a mob in the southern Iraq town of Majar-al-Kabir. More Americans were killed in ambushes. The coalition post-war death toll rose to ten Britons and fifty-two Americans.

Liverpool won the 2008 European Capital of Culture, narrowly beating Newcastle/Gateshead.

John Prescott gave two fingers to the media. He also gave the go-ahead to English devolution referenda in the North-West, North-East and Yorkshire & Humberside regions.

Alan Milburn quit the Cabinet, claiming he wanted to spend more time with his young family. Reid replaced him as Health Secretary ('Fuck, it's not Health?' he was reported to have said when summoned by Blair). Estelle Morris returned to the government as an arts minister. Lord Irvine left as Lord Chancellor. Environment minister Michael Meacher was sacked. Alistair Darling took charge of both Transport and the Scottish Office. Lord Falconer became Secretary of State for Constitutional Affairs. Peter Hain was made Leader of the Commons. He was swiftly forced to withdraw a call for an increase in top-rate income tax.

An unprecedented row flared up between the government and the BBC over reporter Andrew Gilligan's claims to prove that Downing Street did 'sex up' the Iraq dossier. Alastair Campbell told the Foreign Affairs Select Committee that the BBC reports were biased and unsourced. Gilligan threatened to sue the new deputy Leader of the Commons, Phil Woolas.

July
Former prime ministerial consort Denis Thatcher died.

Labour MPs rebelled over foundation hospitals, cutting the government's majority to thirty-five, the lowest during the Blair years and even tighter than the Iraq votes.

The UK clashed with the United States over unreliable evidence that Saddam had been trying to buy uranium from African nations.

Defence scientist David Kelly was outed as the possible mole behind the BBC claim that No. 10 had sexed up the 'dodgy dossier' on weapons of mass destruction. Kelly, who had inspected weapons sites in several UN tours of Iraq, was fiercely grilled by the Foreign Affairs Select Committee. Three days later, while Blair was receiving eighteen standing ovations during a speech in Washington, Kelly apparently killed himself in woodland close to his Oxfordshire home. His death sparked calls for the immediate sacking of Alastair Campbell and Geoff Hoon.

Rail regulator Tom Winsor said that the west coast main line upgrade might be delayed further to save £1 billion.

A relationship between former Tory leadership hopeful John Redwood and his assistant, ex-model Nikki Page, was revealed.

Saddam's sons Uday and Qusay, both regarded as butchers, were killed in a shoot-out with American forces after an informant pinpointed their hiding place. Pictures of their bloody corpses were broadcast across the world.

August
Lord Hutton opened his inquiry into the death of David Kelly. Downing Street spokesman Tom Kelly briefed that Dr Kelly was a 'Walter Mitty' fantasist, sparking a new row as the scientist was buried. During the Hutton inquiry's first week, Andrew Gilligan defended his story but an internal BBC memo judged that his strong investigative journalism was 'marred by flawed reporting'. A tape recording of Kelly by *Newsnight*'s Susan Watts contradicted evidence that he had given to the select committee.

Watts also attacked the BBC for 'pressurising' her in a bid to back up the Gilligan story. The inquiry also heard that Geoff Hoon overrode civil service advice and insisted that Kelly give evidence in public.

Blair overtook Clement Attlee's record for the longest continuous service by a Labour Prime Minister – then flew off on holiday to Cliff Richard's Barbados home.

Peter Mandelson took up kick-boxing.

Former Ugandan despot Idi Amin died.

Three British soldiers were killed in Basra while in a hired taxi.

During the second week of the Hutton inquiry it emerged that No. 10 chief of staff Jonathan Powell had written the previous September that the dossier 'does nothing to demonstrate a threat, let alone an imminent threat, from Saddam'. Alastair Campbell denied that he had any 'input, output or influence' on the inclusion in the dossier of the claim that Saddam could deploy missiles against Israel in forty-five minutes. His diary revealed that Hoon had offered Dr Kelly a 'plea bargain'. No. 10 press aide Godric Smith disclosed that Campbell suggested taking Kelly's name to a newspaper. The inquiry also heard of Kelly's premonition in February that if the Iraq war went ahead he would 'probably be found dead in the woods'. Campbell resigned, to be replaced by David Hill, but kept an advisory role alongside Mandelson. In evidence to the inquiry Blair accepted responsibility for the outing of Kelly and agreed that the government's reputation had been tarnished.

Two terrorist car bombs killed around fifty and injured 200 in Bombay.

'I'm meant to be the bloke who walks around looking like he's going to club a baby seal.' – John Prescott.

September

David Kelly's widow, Janice, told Lord Hutton that he had been 'disturbed, dejected and broken-hearted' by his treatment from the Ministry of Defence. She blamed Geoff Hoon. Intelligence official Brian Jones said that the dossier 'over-egged' the threat posed by Saddam Hussein. A scientist identified only as 'Mr A' said of the dodgy dossier: 'Let's hope it turns into tomorrow's chip wrappers.'

The new director of public prosecutions, Ken Macdonald, said that government plans for longer jail sentences were 'grotesque'.

Up to 2,000 more British troops were scheduled for deployment in Iraq, bringing the total cost of the war and its aftermath to date to £9.2 billion. A Westminster inquiry found that the Joint Intelligence Committee had warned Blair that an invasion of Iraq would increase the terrorist threat to Britain.

Teenager Sharon Finnell's Jack Russell terrier, Jack, relieved himself on the PM's Daimler during a visit to Northampton. She said: 'It was very naughty of him because my mum votes Labour.'

The TUC gave Gordon Brown an ovation of just fifteen seconds. Labour lost its first by-election since 1997 when 29-year-old Liberal Democrat Sarah Teather overturned a 13,000 majority to take Brent East. The government's parliamentary majority was cut to 163.

A government plan to bar all peers convicted of serious offences from sitting in the Upper House suggested that Jeffrey Archer would be stripped of his title.

Cherie Blair's guru Carole Caplin lost her 'key' to Downing Street and expressed fears that she was being bugged.

Alastair Campbell was forced to give Hutton his diary, in which he wrote: 'Geoff Hoon and I agreed that it would fuck Gilligan if that [Kelly] was his source.' Jeremy Gompertz, QC for the Kelly family, accused Hoon of hypocrisy, bullying and lying and said that the decision to out the scientist was a 'cynical abuse of power'. After twenty-four days of evidence from seventy-five witnesses, plus more than 10,000 pages of documentation, the Hutton inquiry closed.

Charles Kennedy told the Lib Dem conference that they offer 'the only credible challenge to the government'. He said that Blair was 'tarnished for good'.

At the Labour conference Blair told his party: 'I can only go one way. I do not have a reverse gear.' He failed to mention Gordon

Brown once. Brown's speech, pledging full employment, was seen as a leadership bid. The government lost votes on foundation hospitals but John Reid ignored them. A revolt over Iraq was averted when the platform refused to allow a separate debate and after former left-winger Ann Clwyd delivered a tearful speech on refugees. Andrew Smith floated the idea of a lump sum for pensioners who work on and don't claim their state pension.

October

Robin Cook said in his memoirs that Tony Blair faced near-mutiny, led by David Blunkett, within the Cabinet over his Iraq war plans. He claimed that Blair bought them off by agreeing to a full Commons debate. No. 10 denied the claim.

At the Tory conference Iain Duncan Smith said: 'The quiet man is here to stay, and he's turning up the volume.' But his pugnacious speech, in which he branded Blair a liar, failed to stem the growing tide against his leadership. Ken Clarke told a fringe meeting that he would not serve in a Cabinet under Duncan Smith. The shadow Cabinet unveiled plans to create sheriffs and to put asylum-seekers on some (unnamed) remote island.

Bereaved families boycotted the service of remembrance for the Iraq war dead.

Terminator film star Arnold Schwarzenegger was elected governor of California, by some estimates the world's sixth largest economy.

Duncan Smith threatened to sue over allegations that he improperly paid his wife Betsy £18,000 a year out of the leader's office secretarial allowance, provided by the taxpayer. He called those plotting against him 'the cowards in the shadows'. Parliamentary standards watchdog Sir Philip Mawer launched an investigation after *Newsnight* reporter Michael Crick presented him with a dossier.

The Transport Select Committee reported that passengers on over-crowded rail services were treated like 'sardines'.

Blair suffered an irregular heartbeat and was whisked from Chequers to Hammersmith Hospital, sparking questions about his longevity as PM. He blamed strong coffee. The scare did not stop him flying to Belfast to unveil, with the Republic's Bertie Ahern, another 'historic breakthrough' in the stalled peace process. But despite guarantees on decommissioning from Gerry Adams and the IRA, David Trimble pulled the plug. He claimed that weapons-inspector John de Chastelain had not furnished enough information on what was claimed to be the biggest act of IRA disarmament in thirty years.

The Lords again scuppered attempts to ban fox-hunting by voting in favour of regulated hunts.

At least twenty-five Tory MPs called a no-confidence vote on Duncan Smith. He vowed to fight on but lost 90-75 and had no option but to stand down. He said: 'It has been an immense honour to lead this great party – and to be the first, the first fully elected leader of the voluntary party and by the full membership.'

Potential candidates Ken Clarke and David Davis rallied behind Michael Howard to ensure a one-horse race.

Post-boxes were sealed as wildcat strikes by postal workers spread across the country. That dispute was settled but fire-fighters again threatened a walk-out over staggered pay rises sanctioned by John Prescott.

November

Michael Howard was confirmed unopposed as Tory leader. He said he would rule from the centre and claimed to have 'mellowed'. Michael Portillo refused a post and announced that he was quitting politics for good. Howard unveiled a 'slimmed-down' twelve-strong shadow Cabinet plus Iain Duncan Smith, William Hague, John Major and Ken Clarke as 'advisors'. The party decided to sell Conservative Central Office in the hopes of raising £6 million.

The government announced a ban on youngsters carrying or using fireworks.

Sixteen US soldiers were killed when a Chinook helicopter was downed by rocket fire near the insurgents' stronghold of Fallujah. Five days later another Chinook was downed, killing six. A week after that two Black Hawk helicopters collided after one was hit by a missile, killing seventeen. Those deaths took the US toll since the start of the Iraq war to 422.

In Saudi Arabia suicide bombers devastated a residential com-pound in Riyadh, killing eighteen and wounding 122. Another suicide attack killed at least thirty-one, including eighteen Italian peace-keepers and five children in British-controlled al-Nasiriyah in Iraq. At least twenty were killed and 303 injured when car bombs exploded outside two synagogues in Istanbul.

It emerged that a Cumbrian hairdresser called Ronnie Campbell had received e-mails – intended for his MP namesake – from Tony Blair asking for advice while preparing his conference speech.

David Blunkett announced that from 2006 all foreign nationals would be required to carry ID cards. The following year everyone applying for a passport or a driving licence would have to provide iris recognition and fingerprint data stored in microchips. The plan was seen as introducing a national ID card by the back door.

President Bush visited Britain amid a massive security operation but was met by largely peaceful demonstrations. Laura Bush refused to curtsey to the Queen. Blair took the President to the Dun Cow Inn in his constituency, where they ate fish, chips and mushy peas. He did not, however, take him to his local, Trimdon Labour Club. A regular said: 'There's nowt but beer here.'

Suicide bomb attacks, timed to coincide with the Bush visit, hit the British consulate and the HSBC bank in Istanbul, leaving twenty-seven dead, including the British consul, and up to 500 injured.

The Lords repeatedly rejected foundation hospitals and the government's Commons majority on the issue was slashed to seventeen. Whips finally pushed the legislation through on the last sitting day before the Queen's Speech. John Reid reacted to claims that it would create a two-tier NHS with the words 'utter bollocks'.

Three-year-old Leo Blair gave President Chirac a signed photo of himself.

The Queen's Speech included student top-up fees, legal rights for same-sex partners, streamlined appeals for rejected asylum-seekers, emergency powers to tackle terrorists, the abolition of Lords seats for the ninety-two remaining hereditary peers, the outlawing of the removal of body parts without family consent, a register of spouse-beaters and a protection fund for victims of failed company pension schemes. Reading it out, the Queen referred to the 'National Hunt Service'.

Blair appeared in the cartoon show *The Simpsons*. Homer mistook him for Mr Bean.

In the Northern Ireland Assembly Ian Paisley's Democratic Unionists became the biggest party with thirty seats, overtaking the Ulster Unionists' twenty-seven. Sinn Fein took twenty-four seats but the other main nationalist party, the SDLP, slumped six to eighteen. The Good Friday agreement appeared on the brink of collapse.

December

Labour MP Chris Bryant posted pictures of himself in his underpants on a gay dating website.

Almost 160 Labour MPs signed a Commons motion demanding a rethink on top-up fees. Tony Blair insisted that he would not back down. Michael Howard told him: 'This grammar school boy is not going to take any lessons from a public schoolboy on the importance of children from less privileged backgrounds gaining access to university.'

Lord Falconer revealed that Blair considered lowering the voting age to sixteen.

Gordon Brown, in his pre-Budget report, threw a £400 million lifeline to local authorities and admitted that borrowing this year would be £10 billion above his £27 billion forecast.

Geoff Hoon signalled further defence cuts and admitted that British troops had been sent into the Iraqi deserts wearing the wrong boots.

Saddam Hussein was captured in a 'rat hole' near his home town of Tikrit. After telling his people to fight to the death, and although armed, he gave himself up meekly.

Libya's Colonel Gaddafi agreed to destroy his weapons of mass destruction in a deal brokered by Blair.

Up to 50,000 were killed and 100,000 left homeless when an earthquake devastated the ancient city of Bam in southern Iran.

In the New Year Honours, coach Clive Woodward was knighted

and the entire England rugby squad received honours for their World Cup victory. Other recipients of gongs included Mick Jagger and David Beckham.

2004

Spin doctors and Cabinet ministers tumbled as the ongoing carnage in Iraq took its toll on Blair.

January
Tony Blair, in his New Year message, said: 'This is no time to turn the clock back, no time to coast, no time to falter with the job only half done.'

The PM flew to Basra to meet the troops. The Bishop of Durham, Tom Wright, said: 'For Bush and Blair to go to Iraq together was like a bunch of white vigilantes going into Brixton to stop drug-dealing.' Lord Hutton delayed his report after Downing Street sent in more submissions.

The royal coroner called in Scotland Yard to reinvestigate Princess Diana's death.

The government announced plans to create 'super traffic wardens' with powers to fine motorists.

'Dr Death', Harold Shipman, killed himself in prison. Home

Secretary David Blunkett said he would have liked to crack open a bottle to celebrate.

Liberal Democrat frontbencher Jenny Tonge was sacked after saying she might have considered becoming a suicide bomber.

Blair offered rebels concessions on student top-up fees, including more aid for poorer students and write-offs after twenty-five years. But he still saw his 161 majority cut to five in a Commons revolt.

Lord Hutton's report on the 'dodgy dossier' was leaked to the *Sun*. He exonerated Blair, Alastair Campbell and Geoff Hoon but condemned the BBC. Critics branded it a whitewash, but nevertheless corporation chairman Gavyn Davies, director-general Greg Dyke and reporter Andrew Gilligan all quit. Acting chairman Lord Ryder issued a grovelling apology.

February

Alastair Campbell embarked on a touring stage show, describing himself as a 'take-no-prisoners control freak'.

Tony Blair appointed former Cabinet Secretary Lord Butler to head a new inquiry into the intelligence which led Britain into war in Iraq. The Lib Dems boycotted it because its remit did not include political decisions.

Twenty illegal Chinese immigrants died while gathering cockles for gang masters on the treacherous Morecambe Sands. David Blunkett signalled that the government would regulate gang masters. Tory MP Ann Winterton was stripped of the party whip after she cracked a joke about the tragedy.

The National Audit Office slammed the Criminal Records Bureau, saying that it couldn't protect children and vulnerable adults because it was unable to access Customs and British Transport Police records – anyone investigated for porn or drug smuggling could be cleared to work with children.

The government gave the go-ahead for a £2.2 billion school building programme.

Tory leader Michael Howard called the British National Party a 'bunch of thugs' in Burnley, where they had seven council seats.

In Belfast, Jane Crudden, a 105-year-old Catholic with eleven children and forty-four grandchildren, was injured when a loyalist gang threw bricks through her window.

March

Tony Blair said he would never err on the side of caution over terrorism. A series of bombs at a crowded Madrid railway station killed 200 and injured around 1,400. Basque separatists were blamed but suspicion fell on al-Qaida. Five of the nine Britons held at Guantanamo Bay were returned after two years' incarceration and cleared of terrorism after just two days of questioning by British police and security officers.

Liverpool Labour MP Peter Kilfoyle featured on TV's *Welcome to the Real World* helping to run a shoot at a posh Scottish estate.

He revealed that he turned against blood sports after shooting kangaroos in Australia.

Gordon Brown's Budget put cigarettes up 8p and petrol 2p per litre, and included a £252 a week minimum income guarantee for families with at least one child, the merger of Customs and Inland Revenue with the loss of 10,500 jobs and a promise to disperse 20,000 civil service jobs to the regions.

The NHS officially became the world's third largest employer, after the Chinese army and the Indian railways.

Charles Kennedy became the target of a whispering campaign suggesting he was ill through drink at the Lib Dems' spring conference in Southport.

Blair met Colonel Gaddafi in Tripoli.

Iain Duncan Smith was cleared by the Parliamentary Commissioner over payments made to his wife Betsy.

The government finally pushed through the student top-up tuition fees Bill despite another revolt.

April

Immigration minister Beverley Hughes was forced to quit over her claim that eastern Europeans were given easy access to Britain as official policy. She insisted she had been 'neither incompetent nor dishonest'. Her boss, David Blunkett, said it was the worst day of his political life.

Shi'ite followers of the extremist cleric Muqtada al-Sadr rebelled in southern Iraq while Sunni resistance elsewhere escalated. Four US workers were killed and publicly mutilated. More than 200 Iraqis were killed and 1,000 reported injured during ferocious fighting in Fallujah. The Americans bombed a mosque. Exactly a year after the fall of Saddam, the death toll among Allied military personnel reached 751, comprising 649 US (511 since the war supposedly ended), 58 UK (25 post-war) and 44 others.

Blair convinced Bush to eventually hand over governance of Iraq to the United Nations. One American was taken hostage, three Japanese hostages were released and an Italian hostage was murdered. An uneasy ceasefire was agreed in Fallujah. And fifty-two former senior diplomats said that Blair's strategy in Iraq and the Middle East was 'doomed'.

The world was shocked by pictures of US soldiers torturing and sexually abusing naked Iraqi prisoners in Abu Ghraib jail. An investigation was launched into allegations of similar mistreatment by British soldiers.

President Bush backed an Israeli plan to give up Gaza but retain key parts of the West Bank. The Palestinians said that the much-vaunted road map to peace was dead.

Almost 100,000 civil servants joined a two-day strike for better pay. Tony Blair performed a U-turn and agreed in principle to a referendum on the EU constitution. Blunkett published the ID card Bill. The Archbishop of Canterbury claimed that Blair's administration had lost public trust.

May

Ten more countries joined the European Union, sparking more immigration fears in Britain.

Daily Mirror photographs allegedly showing an Iraqi prisoner being beaten and kicked by British soldiers proved to be doctored, leading to the resignation of editor Piers Morgan. But the storm over US treatment of detainees grew as more pictures were published from Abu Ghraib. One showed 21-year-old Lynndie England holding a naked prisoner by a dog leash. US military sources revealed that two detainees were murdered at the prison and predicted even more shocking images to come in video footage. US Defence Secretary Donald Rumsfeld made only a half-hearted apology. Tony Blair denied that he or any UK minister had been informed of the allegations, but it emerged that foreign minister Bill Rammell had been told two months earlier by the International Red Cross. A 26-year-old American contractor was beheaded on video in revenge for US abuse of prisoners.

Blair provoked accusations of cronyism by appointing John Scarlett, who let the government off the hook in the Hutton inquiry, as head of MI6.

Polls put Labour at their lowest level for seventeen years – down two points to 32 per cent, while the Tories rose two points to 36 per cent.

Gordon Brown and John Prescott held a secret meeting about Blair's future in the car park of the Loch Fyne oyster bar, it was alleged.

Blair was hit by one of two purple powder-filled condoms thrown from the VIPs' gallery during Prime Minister's Question Time by Fathers4Justice activist Ron Davis. Speaker Michael J. Martin ruled that only his guests would be allowed in that gallery, comprising the front rows of the Strangers' Gallery and separated from the rest by a glass screen. The scare sparked a massive security review of the Palace of Westminster.

John Prescott was blamed for a postal voting fiasco in the upcoming local government and European elections, with seven million ballot forms arriving late.

June

The government drew up a secret plan to prevent a repeat of the 2000 fuel revolt as Budget price rises were due to take effect. But protestors halted a national demonstration after Gordon Brown agreed to hold back the 2p a litre increase announced in March.

Ronald Reagan died.

Health Secretary John Reid caused outrage when he said that for many poor single parents smoking is the only pleasure they get.

Labour was beaten into third place in the local government elections, losing 464 seats and eight councils. The Tories gained 263 seats and the Lib Dems 132. Tony Blair acknowledged that Iraq was a major factor. Ken Livingstone made it back home in London.

Blair suffered another shock with the European elections, but Michael Howard was hit by a surge in support for the UK Independence Party. Overall the Tories lost seven seats and Labour five with UKIP gaining nine and the Lib Dems one. The Conservatives got 28 per cent of the vote, Labour 22 per cent and UKIP and the Lib Dems 18 per cent apiece.

Iraqi power was transferred two days early to an interim administration led by Iyad Allawi. Saddam Hussein was brought before a special court in chains to face charges of crimes against humanity. He insisted he was still President and that the court was illegal.

July

A US Senate committee found that CIA intelligence on Saddam Hussein's supposed weapons of mass destruction was wrong and/or largely uncorroborated. Tony Blair said: 'I have to accept that we have not found them – we may not find them.' The Butler inquiry found that pre-war intelligence was 'seriously flawed' but blamed no individuals.

Transport Secretary Alistair Darling unveiled plans for a new M6 toll motorway between Manchester and Birmingham. He also announced that the Strategic Rail Authority was to be axed after just four years, with the government taking control but with more powers to local transport executives.

The Chancellor's spending review promised more civil service transfers, but also overall staff cuts of 104,000. His package included more for health, education, housing and the intelligence services.

The Public Accounts Select Committee recommended the scrapping of most 'outdated' honours with the OBE replaced by an Order of British Excellence.

The Lib Dems took Leicester South with a 21.5 per cent swing and reduced Labour's majority in Birmingham Hodge Hill to just 460 with a 26 per cent swing. The Tories polled a poor third place in both by-election contests.

John Prescott was forced to ditch plans for referenda on regional assemblies in the North-West and Yorkshire & Humberside, although a North-East devolution poll would go ahead.

Peter Mandelson made his third comeback when Blair appointed him a European Commissioner.

'We will reduce and probably eliminate the homeless by 2008.' – John Prescott.

August
Sinn Fein's Gerry Adams said: 'I think that political unionism uses the IRA and the issue of IRA arms as an excuse. I think that republicans need to be prepared to remove that excuse.'

Thirteen terrorist suspects were rounded up, including one 'significant' al-Qaida figure.

John Prescott helped to rescue kayaker Graham Cook while on holiday.

A-level passes rose for the twenty-second year running, topping 96 per cent.

Allegations were made that Home Secretary David Blunkett had had a three-year affair with married *Spectator* publisher Kimberley Quinn.

A freak flood devastated Boscastle in Cornwall.

Margaret Thatcher's son, Sir Mark Thatcher, was arrested in South Africa over alleged involvement in an Equatorial Guinea coup plot. He faced up to fifteen years in prison, but his mother provided £160,000 bail.

September
More than 320 people, at least half of them children, were killed during the botched rescue by Russian security forces of 1,200 held for fifty-two hours by Chechen terrorists at a school in Beslan.

Andrew Smith quit as Work and Pensions Secretary and was replaced by Alan Johnson. Alan Milburn returned to take charge of election campaigns, much to Gordon Brown's fury. Ian McCartney survived as party chairman despite a vicious whispering campaign.

Fathers4Justice campaigner Jason Hatch, dressed as Batman, spent five hours on a ledge at Buckingham Palace, resulting in a security row.

The government signalled that the Hunting Bill would be rushed through with a ban enforced two years after Royal Assent, apart from hare-coursing, which would become illegal after three months. Eight pro-hunt protestors invaded Westminster and five managed to reach the floor of the Commons chamber, interrupting proceedings. The Bill was passed with a majority of 190.

Lord Bragg claimed that Tony Blair came close to quitting earlier in the year through personal and family pressure, causing a frenzy of speculation. Cherie Blair, on the *Richard and Judy* show to promote her book on other prime ministerial spouses, denied it. She embarked on a worldwide tour to promote her book and reportedly earned around £500,000 from speaking engagements in locations ranging from Washington to Auckland.

Charles Kennedy told the Lib Dem conference that they were ready for government.

Liverpool engineer Ken Bigley was kidnapped in Iraq by Islamic extremists. He pleaded for his life on video after two American fellow-hostages were beheaded. Blair and Jack Straw told the Bigley family that they could not negotiate with terrorists.

At the Labour conference rock star Bono compared Blair and Brown to Lennon and McCartney. Brown said that Labour was the only party which could be trusted with the economy. Blair admitted that Iraq divided the country but stopped short of saying sorry. He said: 'I cannot in all sincerity apologise for ousting Saddam. The world is a better place with him in prison than in power.' A conference stitch-up involving back-room deals with unions defeated an anti-war motion setting a date for British withdrawal.

October

Tony Blair went from the conference to hospital for his heart condition and a 'routine' operation. He declared that he planned to serve a third term as PM but not a fourth, sparking claims that he would be a lame duck leader. It emerged that he and Cherie had bought a £3.6 million house in Connaught Square, near Hyde Park.

Former broadcaster Robert Kilroy-Silk bid to become UKIP leader. Yorkshire millionaire Paul Sykes, who had bankrolled UKIP, announced that he was moving back to the Tories.

Michael Howard, at the Tory conference, summarised his priorities in ten words: 'School discipline, more police, cleaner hospitals, lower taxes, controlled immigration.'

Ken Bigley was beheaded after twenty-one days in captivity. His family were split between those who believed the government did all it could to save him and his brother Paul, who said that Blair had 'blood on his hands'. Tory MP and *Spectator* editor Boris Johnson attacked Liverpool for 'mawkish sentimentality' over Bigley and the Hillsborough football disaster. He went to the city to apologise but failed to do so and was called a 'self-centred, pompous twit' by Paul Bigley.

A report warned of a £78 billion pensions black hole with twelve million people not saving enough for their old age. MPs' annual expenses and allowances topped £78 million.

The Black Watch were part of an 850-strong British force sent to protect US troops in the Fallujah war zone. Geoff Hoon said they would be back by Christmas.

Radio DJ John Peel died. Blair described him as a 'one-off'.

Blair signed the European constitution and signalled a referendum in eighteen months.

November
The government survived two backbench rebellions over super-casinos and smacking children.

Michael Howard, celebrating his first anniversary as Tory leader, admitted that as a schoolboy he skipped some lessons to play snooker.

The North-East referendum rejected a regional assembly by almost four to one, killing devolution in the other English regions. Asked to apologise for the fiasco, John Prescott replied: 'You must be joking.'

Boris Johnson was sacked from the Tory front bench for lying about his four-year affair with journalist Petronella Wyatt.

Five Black Watch soldiers were killed in Iraq. The regiment's commander, Colonel James Cowan, said in a leaked e-mail:

'I hope the government knows what it has got itself into.' Fallujah fell to American forces after a pounding in which 1,000 insurgents were believed killed.

The health White Paper said that smoking should be banned in enclosed public places, restaurants and pubs which serve food.

Labour MSP Lord Watson of Invergowrie was accused of setting fire to a hotel. After attending the Scottish Politician of the Year Awards he demanded more drink from staff at Prestonfield House, Edinburgh, and they reluctantly gave him a bottle. CCTV caught him setting curtains alight after other guests had left. He later pleaded guilty to wilful fire-raising and was sentenced to sixteen months.

The Parliament Act was used to pass the Hunting Bill with a ban to be imposed in February.

The Queen's Speech was dominated by law-and-order issues, including ID cards, spot fines for low-level crime, compulsory drug-testing and anti-terror courts sitting without a jury.

David Blunkett was put on the rack when former mistress Kimberley Quinn claimed he helped speed up her nanny's visa application. She claimed that DNA testing proved her first child was his and said she believed he was also the father of her unborn child, due in February.

Jack Straw and Peter Mandelson faced difficult questions about the failed Equatorial Guinea coup. Sir Mark Thatcher, on bail, said he now knew what a corpse floating downstream felt like.

December

David Blunkett won an early court hearing for his child access case against Kimberley Quinn, ignoring her husband's plea to leave her alone due to ill health and pregnancy. Blunkett slagged off most of his Cabinet colleagues in a taped interview with his biographer. An aide said that Blunkett was having a bad day and 'even Mother Theresa would have got both barrels'. Blunkett resigned after the Budd inquiry found an e-mail which indicated that the nanny's visa application had been fast-tracked. The instruction was 'no special favours but slightly quicker'. In the following reshuffle Charles Clarke became Home Secretary and Ruth Kelly was made Education Secretary.

Former welfare minister Frank Field lost his bid to prosecute a young thug who threatened him outside his Westminster flat.

TV and film comic actor Rowan Atkinson slammed a government bill to penalise those who poke fun at religion.

The Law Lords ruled that holding terrorist suspects without trial was unlawful. Clarke said they would not be released.

More than 125,000 died and many more were missing when an earthquake off Sumatra caused tsunamis which devastated Indonesia, Thailand, India, the Andaman and Nicobar Islands, Sri Lanka, the Maldives and Somalia. A huge international aid mission was launched.

2005

A third election victory was followed by a terrorist blitz on London and a new Despatch Box opponent for Blair.

January
The Asian tsunami death toll topped 160,000, including more than ninety Britons. The British public gave over £100 million to the disaster fund and the government promised to match that amount.

Squabbling between Tony Blair and Gordon Brown intensified as a book claimed that Blair had reneged on a promise to stand down the previous autumn. Both men unveiled identical strategies to tackle African poverty at the same time but at different venues. Labour MP Frank Field urged that the Chancellor be sacked for disloyalty.

A row erupted when Prince Harry went to a party wearing a Nazi armband.

The government was slammed for its 'binge-drinking' Bill, allowing premises to stay open twenty-four hours a day. Ministers promised a purge on bad pubs, alcohol disorder zones and 'three strikes and you're barred' for persistent drunks.

Film of Iraqi looters being abused was shown at the court martial of four British soldiers. Sixty per cent of the Iraqi electorate defied bombers and gunmen to vote in the country's first free elections for a generation.

February

Tony Blair declared war on 'sicknote culture' and announced curbs on incapacity benefit.

Recently retired broadcaster John Sergeant's memoirs claimed that Frank Field advised Margaret Thatcher to quit and back John Major. Field also called for MPs to decide the Queen's successor so that Prince Charles could be vetoed. A row blazed over whether the upcoming civil wedding of Charles and Camilla was lawful.

Another ex-TV man, Robert Kilroy-Silk, left UKIP and formed his own party, Veritas.

The fox-hunting ban came into force . . . ninety-one foxes were 'legally' killed on the first day.

Ministers announced the uprating of the national minimum wage from £4.85 an hour to £5.05 from October, with the promise of a £1.30 rise the following year.

March

The government's majority was cut to fourteen by rebellion against efforts to speed through new anti-terror laws. Rebels, Lords and Tories forced ministers to back down by inserting a 'sunset' clause after a marathon thirty-hour session, meaning that the laws must be regularly renewed by Parliament.

Michael Howard used the case of Warrington grandmother Margaret Dixon, who had seen seven shoulder operations cancelled, to highlight failings in the NHS.

Gordon Brown's Budget was aimed at grey voters, with £200 council tax rebates for pensioners, £200 winter fuel payments and free off-peak local bus travel.

Tony Blair accused the Tories of planning £35 billion public spending cuts. The Tories accused Labour of planning £35 billion tax rises. Tory deputy chairman Howard Flight was sacked by Michael Howard after he told a private meeting that their tax cuts would go further.

Former Labour premier James Callaghan died on the eve of his 93rd birthday and eleven days after his wife Audrey.

April

After a delay caused by Pope John Paul's death, Blair confirmed 5 May as the general election date. Campaigning was officially suspended for the Pope's funeral, but Michael Howard launched a focus on immigration. Blair suggested that Brown was the 'best-ever' Chancellor in an apparent bid to heal recent rifts. The campaign proper opened on 10 April.

Liberal Democrat leader Charles Kennedy became the father of baby Donald James. He took two days' paternity leave and then fluffed a press conference, claiming that he had not had much sleep.

Cherie Blair told party supporters at a London fund-raising event to give ex-Labour MP George Galloway a 'bloody nose'. Galloway was standing in an east London seat for the new left-wing Respect party.

Labour chairman Ian McCartney said: 'My wife says I have the charm of Hugh Grant, the looks of a young Al Pacino, the screen presence of Tom Cruise – all wrapped up in the body of Danny De Vito.'

At the launch of the party manifestos Labour unveiled 272 promises, ranging from training places for all sixteen-year-olds to better parish councils. The Tories focused on immigration and school discipline, but internal polls suggested that immigration backfired as a populist issue. The Lib Dems concentrated on scrapping student tuition fees and abolishing council tax. Blair was hectored by Jeremy Paxman. John Prescott told a south Wales journalist: 'Bugger off. Get on your bus, you amateur.' National newspapers were bypassed by Labour campaign managers and local events were packed with carefully chosen 'ordinary voters'. The BBC's Nick Robinson asked whether Blair had met a single 'ordinary voter' during the entire campaign, while Sky's Adam Boulton referred to Blair's 'sterile environment'.

Leaks suggested that Attorney-General Lord Goldsmith had changed his mind, in legal advice, over the legality of the Iraq war. The row put Iraq and Blair's trustworthiness at the centre of the election campaign. The government published Goldsmith's advice in full and Blair said that if people really believed he had lied, they should not vote for him.

May

Labour won the general election but with its majority slashed to sixty-six. In the *Times* Rosie Bennett wrote: 'The stresses and strains of the war and the Hutton inquiry clearly took their toll on Mr Blair.' And her colleague Alice Miles added: 'The second term ended as it had begun, with the PM saying that he now knew what needed to be done to transform Britain's public services and believed he had secured the personal and political wherewithal to do it.' Blair promised to 'listen and learn'. Michael Howard announced he planned to stand down as Conservative leader. Charles Kennedy hailed the best Liberal showing for eighty years, with sixty-two seats. The Tories were left with 197 seats to Labour's 355, nowhere near the breakthrough that earlier polls had suggested. Respected commentator Philip Webster regarded it as a strange campaign with few real winners. He added: 'So a new Parliament began with Mr Blair still in charge and no-one knowing quite how long he would last.' George Galloway won his seat for Respect. Robert Kilroy-Silk took a derisory vote for Veritas and lost his deposit.

Election supremo Alan Milburn stood down from the Cabinet. In the subsequent reshuffle David Blunkett returned as Work and Pensions Secretary, John Reid took command of Defence,

Patricia Hewitt took Health, Ruth Kelly Education and Alan Johnson Trade and Industry. David Miliband was made communities and local government minister.

The Queen's Speech put 'respect and reform' at the top of Blair's third-term agenda. Forty-five bills covered a crackdown on knife crime, a points system for immigrants, pension reform and measures to allow the best schools to take over failing ones.

Blair went to hospital for an injection to ease the pain of a slipped disc. Asked about the treatment, Cherie said: 'Men are never brave.'

George Galloway took on the US Senate in a hearing on Iraq and was judged the winner on points.

French and Dutch referenda said '*non*' and '*nej*' to the proposed new European constitution. Blair admitted that it was now dead.

June

Cherie Blair came under fire for using an official Washington trip to deliver a private lecture, for which she was reportedly paid £30,000. She denied that it was linked to her role as the PM's spouse, even though the event had been billed as an opportunity to meet the 'First Lady of Downing Street'. Tony Blair was also in the US capital but No. 10 insisted: 'If [Cherie] and the PM are in Washington at the same time it is a coincidence.'

Gordon Brown wrote off £22 billion in Third World debt.

A leaked Home Office review targeted toddler tearaways. Frank Field urged that 'families from hell' should be housed in lorry containers.

An EU summit collapsed when Blair refused to give up a £3 billion rebate and Jacques Chirac refused to move on the Common Agricultural Policy.

Cleanliness in NHS hospitals became a big concern thanks to an outbreak of the MRSA infection. Commons financial watchdogs reported that the whole 'superbug' issue was 'shrouded in fog'.

July

The Live8 world-wide concerts focused minds on the plight of Africa. As world leaders gathered for a G8 summit in Gleneagles, the debts of the fifteen poorest nations were wiped out. That did not stop demonstrators clashing violently with police in Edinburgh and besieging the approach roads to the conference.

In Singapore Cherie Blair was described as the 'secret weapon' to win over International Olympic Committee delegates. London did indeed beat Paris to snatch the venue for the 2012 Olympics. The capital rejoiced – until the following morning . . .

7th: British Islamic suicide bombers detonated their packages on three London Underground trains and one bus, killing fifty-two people and injuring 700. Tony Blair flew down from the G8 summit. He said: 'When they try to intimidate us, we will not be intimidated. When they seek to change our country or our way of life, we will not be changed.' The four dead bombers were identified as home-grown, having travelled by train to London via Luton. An inquiry into intelligence failings ahead of the atrocity was launched.

Another terrorist blitz on London was foiled two weeks later when four more bombs failed to go off, again three on the Tube and one on a bus, and the would-be suicide bombers fled. They were swiftly arrested, two in London, one in Birmingham and one in Rome. The following day an innocent Brazilian, Jean Charles de Menezes, was shot five times in the head and killed at Stockwell Tube station by armed police who mistook him for a terrorist suspect. After prevaricating, the Metropolitan Police commissioner, Sir Ian Blair, finally apologised for the tragedy. An inquiry found that the victim was sitting down, unaware he was a suspect, when he was shot, and pressure grew for the commissioner's resignation.

Furious Railtrack shareholders took Stephen Byers to the High Court over his 'back door' renationalisation.

The IRA renounced violence and began further arms decommissioning. Tony Blair said: 'This may be the day when finally, after all the false dawns and dashed hope, peace replaces war, politics replaces terror on the island of Ireland.' Unionists said that they'd heard it all before.

August

Antony Walker, a black eighteen-year-old from Liverpool, was axed to death in a race hate crime. Two men charged with his murder included the brother of a Manchester City footballer. Antony was buried amid emotional scenes and his aunt told local people: 'We didn't know you cared.' Four months later the killers were sentenced to life imprisonment.

Tony Blair announced a crackdown on those who preach hate, including the threatened deportation of Islamic extremists. He said: 'Coming to Britain is not a right and staying here carries with it a duty. That is to share and support the values that sustain the British way of life. Those who break that duty and try and incite or engage in violence against our country or our people have no place here.' Islamic preacher Omar Bakri Mohammed, who fled to Lebanon after reading reports he could be tried for treason, was told he could not return.

Robin Cook died, aged fifty-nine, while walking on a Scottish mountainside with his wife Gaynor. Blair chose not to interrupt his holiday for the funeral. At the service racing pundit John McCririck accused the PM of 'petty vindictiveness'.

Former Cabinet minister Mo Mowlam finally succumbed to cancer and died, aged fifty-one. Northern Ireland civil rights campaigner and former SDLP leader Lord (Gerry) Fitt also died, aged seventy-nine.

September
Ken Clarke launched a Tory leadership bid.

Hurricane Katrina hit the American south, killing up to 10,000 and all but destroying New Orleans. Thousands of refugees fled and Barbara Bush, the President's mother, said that as many were poor, they were probably better off.

A Whitehall report said that Jobcentres were becoming 'war zones' with a 62 per cent increase in attacks on staff. Further reports suggested that the Child Support Agency was in 'meltdown'.

Amicus union leader Derek Simpson said that Tony Blair must go, while the BBC carpeted newsman John Humphrys for an after-dinner speech in which he mocked New Labour.

Charles Kennedy blamed Blair for the ongoing death toll in Iraq after a week of mayhem and the rescue of two British soldiers from local police. He also told the Lib Dem conference that he aimed to squash those who plotted against him and pledged to fight the next election.

Cherie Blair revealed that she had her first kiss, aged seven, with Stephen Smerdon, now a pub landlord. He said: 'If I saw her today I'd kick her backside for naming me like that.'

At the Labour conference in Brighton Blair unveiled a programme for full employment. He lost conference votes on pensions, the privatisation of public services and secondary picketing, but again chose to ignore the defeats. Walter Wolfgang, an 82-year-old who had escaped the Holocaust, was roughly ejected from the conference hall when he heckled Jack Straw over Iraq. He was arrested by police using new anti-terrorist powers but was later released. Straw said that he was furious at the older man's treatment and Blair issued an apology.

David Blunkett was again rocked by sex scandal when his 29-year-old girlfriend Sally Anderson kissed and told.

October
The Tory conference at Blackpool was dominated by the leadership contest. Ken Clarke pressed the right buttons, David Davis performed dismally, while Liam Fox and Sir Malcolm Rifkind proved to be no-hopers . . . but David Cameron wowed the conference audience. Later he faced questions on whether he had ever taken Class A drugs. He insisted that what he did before he entered politics was no-one else's business. Rifkind dropped out of the race, Clarke was defeated in the first ballot of Tory MPs and Fox in the second. Cameron and Davis then faced a six-week battle to woo the 300,000-strong party membership.

More than 28,000 died in earthquakes across Kashmir, India and Afghanistan.

A TV 'farce', *A Very Social Secretary*, chronicled David Blunkett's affair with Kimberley Quinn.

Blair proposed 'sin bins' for problem families and Education Secretary Ruth Kelly said teachers could use 'reasonable force' to control and discipline unruly pupils. A government plan to ban booze on trains and buses was dropped when greeted with widespread ridicule.

November
Blair suffered what many saw as the worst week so far of his

premiership. David Blunkett was forced to quit again, this time over undisclosed outside earnings and shares in DNA Biosciences. Standards Committee chairman Sir Alistair Graham ruled that he had broken the ministerial code. Blunkett was replaced by John Hutton. Within hours the government's majority was cut to just one in a revolt over terror laws. Later Blair was defeated for the first time over efforts to allow the detention without charge of terrorist suspects for up to ninety days, losing a Commons vote by thirty-one. The PM said that it was better to be defeated than to have backed away.

Cherie Blair said that if it had not been for free education she would have ended up a shop worker.

Former UK ambassador to Washington Sir Christopher Meyer wrote in his memoirs that Blair was 'under-briefed and out of his depth' in the run-up to the Iraq war. He was scathing about Cabinet ministers and said that trying to put Defence Secretary Geoff Hoon on the same wavelength as his US opposite number, Donald Rumsfeld, was 'like getting pandas to mate'. Blair reportedly called Meyer a 'complete prick'.

The Licensing Act, allowing 24-hour drinking, came into effect.

December
Gordon Brown's pre-Budget report offered the elderly more help with heating bills over Christmas. He was forced to cut his economic growth forecast to 1.75 per cent.

David Cameron took the Tory leadership after trouncing David

Davis by a margin of more than two to one. Cameron promised more 'caring' Conservatism and said of Blair: 'He was the future once.' TV mimic Rory Bremner said he 'does a better Blair than me'. The Tories took an opinion poll lead over Labour for the first time since the height of the anti-war protests.

Dennis Skinner was ordered out of the Commons chamber after suggesting shadow Chancellor George Osborne took cocaine.

2006

Blair inflicted his own Night of the Long Knives and survived a coup plot, but his last full calendar year as PM was undermined by the rumbling inquiry into cash for honours.

January

Liberal Democrat leader Charles Kennedy admitted to having had treatment for a drink problem. He said he was 'inundated' with support. But twenty-five of his party's MPs warned they would no longer serve under him and he was forced to quit. Sir Menzies Campbell – dubbed Ming the Merciless – was the first to stand for the leadership, followed by Mark Oaten, party president Simon Hughes and Chris Huhne, who had been an MP for just eight months. Oaten pulled out of the race and resigned as home affairs frontbencher after admitting to a three-year relationship with a male prostitute. He later blamed a 'midlife crisis' triggered by going bald. The row led Hughes, who had originally won his Bermondsey seat on a 'straight' ticket, to come out as bisexual. Some pollsters reckoned public support for the party fell to 13 per cent.

New Conservative leader David Cameron ditched the party's previous manifesto and described the NHS as 'one of the greatest gifts we enjoy as British citizens', promising that it would be safe in Tory hands. Similar U-turns followed over green taxes, grammar schools and same-sex partnerships.

Education Secretary Ruth Kelly was in trouble after an admitted paedophile was cleared by her office to work as a PE teacher. She compounded the crisis by admitting she had 'no idea' how many paedophile teachers there were. Kelly announced that in future all convicted sex offenders would be banned from working in schools.

Tony Blair launched his 'respect agenda', including wider powers to issue parenting orders, forcing parents to take responsibility for their offspring.

Home Secretary Charles Clarke decided against downgrading the classification of cannabis. He blocked council plans to allow red light zones but approved a scheme to allow small brothels run by prostitutes themselves.

The government called a cull of thousands of grey squirrels to protect the reds. A huge rescue effort for a bottlenose whale lost in the Thames tragically failed.

Cameron told Blair: 'You came into politics to soak the rich and ban the bomb. Now you're sucking up to the rich and dropping bombs.'

George Galloway was voted out of the Big Brother reality TV house after cavorting in a red leotard and playing a pussy cat.

February

Muslims across Europe demonstrated and fire-bombed embassies following the publication of Danish cartoons deemed to be offensive to the Prophet.

Work and Pensions Secretary John Hutton unveiled major reform of the Child Support Agency.

Labour lost the Dunfermline by-election, in Gordon Brown's back yard, with Lib Dem Willie Rennie overturning an 11,000 majority.

The Commons voted overwhelmingly to ban smoking in all workplaces and enclosed public areas, including pubs and private members' clubs.

Al-Qaida terrorists disguised as police bombed the al-Askari shrine in Samarra, one of the most revered Shia sites in Iraq. The collapse of the famous golden dome marked the beginning of a new phase in sectarian violence bordering on all-out civil war. By the end of the day Shia mobs had attacked twenty-seven Sunni mosques.

Blair survived two more revolts over ID cards and terror laws.

March

Culture Secretary Tessa Jowell was cleared of breaching the ministerial code of conduct because her husband did not tell her about a £344,000 gift allegedly paid during an Italian corruption trial.

Menzies Campbell won the Lib Dem leadership contest, with Chris Huhne easily overtaking Simon Hughes to come a respectable second.

John Profumo, 1960s scandal veteran turned charity worker, died aged ninety-one.

Tony Blair was hit by a new sleaze storm over loans for lordships. He admitted that Labour had secretly been lent £14 million to bankroll the 2005 election and that some of the donors had subsequently been nominated for peerages. Party treasurer Jack Dromey slammed Downing Street for keeping him in the dark, and party chairman Ian McCartney revealed he had been told to sign certificates while he was in hospital recovering from a triple heart bypass.

Slobodan Milošević, former Serbian President, died aged sixty-four while on trial for war crimes.

Gordon Brown's tenth Budget included a freeze on champagne duty, free off-peak national bus travel for pensioners, road tax hikes for gas-guzzlers and an extra £585 million in direct payments to schools.

Basque separatists ETA called a permanent ceasefire after a forty-year terrorist campaign.

US Secretary of State Condoleezza Rice faced demonstrations when she visited Merseyside and Burnley as the guest of Jack Straw. Mersey poet Roger McGough pulled out of a

Liverpool Philharmonic concert given in her honour.

April
David Cameron called UKIP members 'fruitcakes, loonies and closet racists'. They threatened to sue.

Police arrested and interrogated former government advisor Des Smith after he allegedly told an undercover reporter that big donations to Tony Blair's flagship city academies would earn a knighthood or peerage. Police also raided the Cabinet Office as part of the loans investigation.

A Labour local election broadcast portrayed Cameron as a chameleon.

Labour accounts revealed that Cherie Blair charged £7,000 for hairdos during the one-month general election campaign.

The Queen celebrated her eightieth birthday.

New Labour's blackest week (again) came out of the blue. Deputy premier John Prescott was forced to admit a two-year affair with his diary secretary, Tracey Temple. Health Secretary Patricia Hewitt had to abandon her speech to the Royal College of Nursing because of heckling. And Charles Clarke had to admit that more than 1,000 convicted foreign criminals, including murderers, rapists and drug-smugglers, had not been deported after completing their sentences. At least five reoffended.

May

Labour was knocked into third place in local council elections, losing most heavily in London and southern England.

Tony Blair responded by butchering most of the top layer of his Cabinet. John Prescott lost most of his responsibilities but kept his title, grace-and-favour homes and other perks. Charles Clarke was sacked as Home Secretary and replaced by John Reid. Jack Straw was demoted to Leader of the Commons and replaced at the Foreign Office by Margaret Beckett. Ruth Kelly lost her stewardship of Education and was replaced by Alan Johnson. Des Browne took over Defence. Geoff Hoon switched from Leader of the Commons to Europe minister. Ian McCartney was sacked as party chairman and replaced by Hazel Blears, but was made a trade minister.

Rebel Labour MPs threatened to force a leadership contest if Blair didn't set a timetable for his departure. Gordon Brown helpfully reminded Blair how Margaret Thatcher had been kicked out by her party. George Galloway suggested that to assassinate Blair could be 'morally justifiable'.

Reid admitted that he had no idea how many illegal immigrants there were in Britain but estimated around 400,000. Cleaners at the Home Office were found to be among them. Reid's problems mounted when it was revealed that an immigration 'sex for passports' scam had been detected, foreign mental patients were being let loose in the community, and more criminals were being allowed to stay rather than suffer deportation. Reid told an inquiry that the Home Office was incompetent and 'not fit for purpose'.

Blair took his Whitsun holidays, leaving Prescott in charge . . . who was pictured playing croquet at Dorneywood, his grace-and-favour country mansion. The row forced Prescott to give the house up.

'My husband always says that I'm a bolshie Scouser.' – Cherie Blair.

June
More than 250 officers raided a London home, searching for a terrorist cell, and shot and wounded suspect Mohammed Abdul Kahar. He and his brother were arrested protesting their innocence, but were later released without charge.

In Iraq, Jordanian terrorist Abu Musab al-Zarqawi, claimed by the CIA to have murdered Ken Bigley, was reported killed.

John Reid investigated the introduction of 'Sarah's Law', whereby parents can find out if convicted paedophiles live in their area, sending a junior minister to the United States, which has equivalent legislation in some states. However, the idea was later shelved. Reid banned child sex offenders from eleven hostels near schools.

Charles Haughey, former Irish premier, died aged eighty.

Gordon Brown approved the next £25 billion Trident nuclear weapons generation.

David Cameron appeared on the Jonathan Ross TV show and

was asked whether he masturbated over pictures of Margaret Thatcher when a teenager. He made no comment. . . and no complaint.

Charles Clarke put the boot into Blair, saying: 'There is a sense of Tony having lost his sense of direction.' David Blunkett told Clarke: 'Bitterness in politics only corrodes those involved in it. Would you please put a sock in it.'

Margaret Beckett revealed her reaction when offered the Foreign Secretaryship: 'One word, and four lettered.'

July
John Prescott stayed at the ranch of US billionaire Philip Anschutz, who wanted to turn the Dome into a super-casino.

More than 200 were killed and 700 injured when seven bomb blasts tore through trains and railway stations during rush hour in Mumbai. Suspected Islamic extremists killed seven in Kashmir a few hours earlier.

David Cameron told the Tories to start hugging hoodies.

Police arrested Labour fund-raiser Lord Levy and detained him for nine hours as part of their cash-for-honours probe. David Blunkett said that people wanted the Met to be 'thorough, not theatrical'.

Israel attacked Lebanon after three of its soldiers were taken hostage. Hezbollah bombed Israeli cities while Israel bombed Beirut and sent troops across the border. Hundreds died in the Israeli blitz, including thirty-seven children in one attack. Tony Blair was criticised for failing to demand a ceasefire.

George W. Bush greeted the PM with the words 'Yo, Blair' during a summit in St Petersburg.

Ministers announced the scrapping of the Child Support Agency and its replacement by a new body with powers to seize property and electronically tag defaulters.

Left-wing Labour MP Peter Kilfoyle had a quadruple bypass and said later: 'The doctors found my heart but couldn't find my wallet.'

August

MSP Tommy Sheridan won his libel case against the *News of the World* over allegations that he was a serial love cheat who used drugs. The newspaper paid him £200,000.

Tony Wright of the Exmoor Foxhounds became the first person to be convicted of illegally hunting with dogs.

Two teenagers were found guilty of killing ten-year-old Damilola Taylor in 2000 in Peckham.

Tony Blair postponed his Barbados holiday to broker a UN ceasefire in Lebanon after the Security Council demanded an end to the conflict between Israel and Hezbollah fighters and for the release of the Israeli soldiers whose kidnapping triggered the war.

Police and security services foiled a terrorist plot to use chemical bombs to blow up several airliners flying from UK airports to America. Twenty-four suspects were arrested and police claimed that, if successful, the plot would have resulted in mass murder on a bigger scale than 9/11. John Reid took charge of the operation, sidelining John Prescott, who was nominally leader while Blair was on holiday. The PM was severely criticised for not returning home while thousands of Britons suffered holiday chaos at airports.

Prescott reportedly told Labour MPs that President Bush was a 'cowboy' and his Lebanon policy was 'crap'.

September

Tony Blair proposed ASBOs for children before they are born.

Fourteen British servicemen were killed when their Nimrod crashed in Afghanistan, the biggest military loss of life in a single incident since the Falklands War.

Labour 'loyalists' signed a letter saying Blair must set a date for his resignation, sparking another leadership crisis. Seven junior members of the government, led by defence minister Tom Watson, resigned. After forty-eight hours of mounting turmoil Blair apologised to voters for internal party warfare and said that he would not be leader by roughly the same time next year. 'I would have preferred to do this in my own way,' he said, adding:

'It has not been New Labour's finest hour.' Gordon Brown pledged his support.

Brown was pictured emerging from a crucial meeting with Blair smiling broadly. . . resulting in an anti-Brown backlash. He was accused of failing to curb supporters planning a coup against Blair. Charles Clarke said he was 'stupid . . . stupid, stupid'. He said that Brown could have distanced himself from the plot 'with a click of his fingers', adding: 'This has been complete madness.' Frank Field waded in, saying that Brown did not have the bottle to be PM. It emerged that Watson had visited Brown's Dunfermline home shortly before the failed coup.

Blair hit back, warning that Labour would be punished by the electorate at the next election if the civil war continued. Visiting a school with Education Secretary Alan Johnson, he told pupils: 'I've brought Alan with me. You've got to have a friend. At least I've got one.' Europe minister Geoff Hoon said that Blair should quit before the May 2007 local government elections 'while he is still popular'.

Labour fund-raiser Lord Levy told police that he was acting on the direct orders of Blair when he secretly obtained £14 million in loans from business leaders. He claimed that the PM hosted dinners and meetings with those who went on to loan cash.

NATO forces launched Operation Medusa in Afghanistan, a drive into the Taliban-infested Panjwayi and Zhari districts, killing more than 1,000 insurgents.

The Tories dropped the torch as their party logo, replacing it with a green smudge representing an oak tree. Lord Tebbit said it looked like 'a bunch of broccoli'.

At the Lib Dem conference leader Sir Menzies Campbell won a vote to drop the party's commitment to a 50p top rate of income tax in favour of higher green taxes. Charles Kennedy was given a standing ovation and pledged his continuing loyalty. Paddy Ashdown castigated him for overshadowing the leader's speech.

John Reid was heckled when he urged Muslim parents in east London to prevent their children being seduced by Islamic extremism.

Brown told the Labour conference that he was proud to have served under Blair. Cherie Blair allegedly called him a liar. Blair said of Cherie: 'At least I don't have to worry about her running off with the bloke next door.' In his swansong conference speech he warned that an Iraqi pull-out would be a 'craven act of cowardice'. Reid's speech was seen as a launch pad for his own leadership bid. John Prescott said sorry to the party and his wife Pauline for his affair. She became tearful when he announced it would be his last conference as deputy leader and deputy premier.

'We have eradicated long-term youth unemployment.' – Tony Blair.

October
David Cameron told the Tory conference that his priority was

the NHS. He gave no promise of tax cuts. Shadow Home Secretary David Davis said: 'David Cameron wants us to hug a hoodie. I support that. The only difference is that I would hug them a little harder and a little longer . . .' Boris Johnson said he would 'get rid of' celebrity cook Jamie Oliver. Cameron said: 'It's been a great week for everyone. Even Boris made it all the way to Tuesday afternoon before he put his foot in it.' Cameron produced an internet blog showing him doing the washing up. Labour MP Siôn Simon produced a spoof version urging viewers to take his wife and kids.

Jack Straw sparked Muslim rage when he revealed that he told women to remove their veils at constituency surgeries, saying: 'I felt uncomfortable about talking to someone face to face who I could not see.'

David Blunkett revealed that he thought he was 'going mad' after his doomed affair with Kimberley Quinn. Former prison service head Martin Narey claimed that Blunkett, when Home Secretary, told him to call in the army to 'machine-gun' prisoners in a 2002 riot. The Blunkett diaries spread blame for his fall on everyone except himself. Ex-chief whip Nick Brown said: 'He is disqualifying himself from consideration as a serious politician.'

Alastair Campbell also confessed that he battled depression during his No. 10 years and that the suicide of Dr David Kelly was a 'personal nightmare'.

Defence chief General Sir Richard Dannatt, a Military Cross holder, enraged Downing Street by saying that British forces in

Iraq should be brought home soon otherwise the conflict could 'break' the army. He said: 'I don't say the difficulties we are experiencing around the world are caused by our presence in Iraq, but undoubtedly our presence in Iraq exacerbates them.' Later he issued a statement saying: 'We don't do surrender.'

The St Andrews agreement on the Northern Ireland peace process was thrashed out over three days of talks involving Tony Blair and Bertie Ahern. The deal paved the way for power-sharing between Democratic Unionist leader Ian Paisley and Sinn Fein President Gerry Adams from 26 March 2007. There were no handshakes between the old enemies.

Former International Development Secretary Clare Short finally quit Labour to continue as an independent MP. She hit out at an 'arrogant, error-prone' government and accused Blair of telling 'half-truths and deceits to get us to war in Iraq'. She added that a hung Parliament would be best for the country. Peter Kilfoyle said: 'No matter how strongly you feel about issues, you should stay inside the party and fight your cause.'

Shadow Chancellor George Osborne was rebuked for telling Gordon Brown: 'You'll make an effing awful Prime Minister.'

Shadow environment minister Gregory Barker left his wife and children for another man, a decorator who had been refurbishing the Barker family home.

Lib Dem Lembit Öpik, formerly engaged to weather forecaster Siân Lloyd, was revealed to be having an affair with 23-year-old

Gabriela Irimia, half of the pop duo the Cheeky Girls. It was later claimed that he lobbied the Home Office to grant a visa extension for his lover. Lloyd said she wouldn't be giving back the Welsh gold engagement ring: 'It's very special to me . . . I wouldn't like to see it on the finger of a Cheeky Girl.'

Parents who fail to control under-ten tearaways could face a fine of up to £3,000, policing minister Tony McNulty warned.

Scotland Yard's inquiry into cash for honours had involved the arrest of three people and the questioning of at least fifty, it emerged. The arrestees were Lord Levy, party donor Sir Christopher Evans and Des Smith, advisor to the government's city academies programme. Those questioned under caution included Downing Street government relations director Ruth Turner and John McTernan, Blair's director of political operations. Others questioned, but not cautioned, included Michael Howard, Ian McCartney and science minister Lord Sainsbury.

NATO attacked Taliban positions in Lakani. During the battle a US gunship strafed shepherds and their families, mistaking them for insurgents. Since June the United States had carried out 2,000 air strikes in Afghanistan compared to eighty-eight in Iraq. During October 245 people were killed in Afghanistan by suicide bombers and roadside bombs. The government defeated an attempt by MPs to set up an inquiry into the Iraq war.

The unnamed police marksman who shot dead Jean Charles de Menezes killed a suspected armed robber in Kent.

November

An Iraqi court sentenced Saddam Hussein to death by hanging for crimes against humanity after a 55-week trial. The specific offence was that he ordered the torture and murder of 148 men and boys in the village of Dujail after his convoy was attacked in 1982. Other crimes still to be counted included the killing of 100,000 Kurds in the north and a similar number of Shias in the south. During the trial he told the court to 'go to hell'. Two days after the sentence he said: 'I call on all Iraqis, Arabs and Kurds, to forgive, reconcile and shake hands.'

George Bush got, in his own words, 'a thumping' in the American mid-term elections, losing control of both the Senate and the House of Representatives. Defence Secretary Donald Rumsfeld immediately resigned, an acknowledgement that the Iraq war and its aftermath was a major factor in the Democrat landslide. Labour enlisted Howard Dean, architect of that victory, to advise them on the run-up to next May's council elections.

Lord Sainsbury quit as science minister but insisted it had nothing to do with the cash-for-honours probe. Since 2002 he had donated £6 million to Labour. He said: 'I am not directly involved in whether peerages were offered for cash. I am not the party's fund-raiser and I have been a peer for nine years so no-one is suggesting I was in the business of trying to buy a peerage.'

BNP leader Nick Griffin celebrated with champagne after being cleared in Leeds of trying to incite racial hatred. The court heard that the BBC filmed him claiming that the Koran told Asian men it was acceptable to rape young English girls. Gordon Brown said that race laws may have to be amended, but John Reid disagreed, arguing for time to allow the new racial hatred law to 'bed in'.

MI5 head Eliza Manningham-Buller revealed that her department had at least 1,600 terrorist suspects under surveillance. She said: 'I wish life were like [the TV series] *Spooks*, where everything is (a) knowable and (b) soluble by six people.'

Gordon Brown said that only he can protect Britain from terrorists.

Reid told drinkers outside a Westminster pub to behave themselves, 'as the prisons are full'.

MPs demanded that Sir Clive Thompson, boss of the collapsed Christmas hamper and voucher firm Farepak, be stripped of his knighthood. More than 150,000 people lost £40 million in cash already paid, blighting their seasonal festivities.

Tony Blair's last Queen's Speech focused on a crackdown on organised crime, tougher controls on illegal and criminal immigrants and an expansion of the security services to combat terrorism – all within John Reid's remit.

Blair signalled his leadership support for 'heavyweight' Gordon Brown, who would be capable of giving 'flyweight' David Cameron a 'big clunking fist'. Cameron said: 'The tragedy of this PM is that he promised so much but delivered so little.'

The government's health watchdog warned that eggs from

abroad were putting millions of Britons at risk, with salmonella bacteria found in one in every thirty boxes imported.

Downing Street blamed the police for leaking details of the cash-for-honours inquiry. Blair was accused of misleading the party's national executive over secret loans. He had previously claimed that donors feared being 'trashed in the media' if they contributed to Labour's 2005 election campaign. But businessman Chai Patel said he initially offered £1.5 million as an outright donation. And Sir Gulam Noon also insisted he had offered to donate £250,000 but was told that a loan would be more acceptable. Metropolitan Police deputy assistant commissioner John Yates signalled that Blair would be quizzed before January on the affair.

Four British soldiers were killed by a bomb as they carried out a river patrol in Basra. Two suicide bombers killed thirty-five would-be police recruits in Baghdad.

The Serious Fraud Squad launched an investigation into a deal approved by Blair to sell a £28 million air traffic control system to Tanzania with backhanders allegedly paid by British Aerospace.

Prisoners accepted undisclosed compensation for being forced to give up drugs while in jail.

The Centre for Economics and Business Research predicted that 4,200 City high-flyers would collect Christmas bonuses worth more than £1 million apiece, 40 per cent more than in 2005. The bankers at Goldman Sachs were paid an average £320,000 each and were dubbed 'the haves and have-yachts'.

Employment minister Margaret Hodge accused Blair of 'moral imperialism' over the war in Iraq, a conflict she also described as his 'big mistake in foreign affairs'. In an interview with David Frost on Aljazeera, Blair appeared to agree that Iraq had been 'pretty much of a disaster'.

A Tory internal document urged the party to drop Winston Churchill as a role model and adopt *Guardian* social affairs correspondent Polly Toynbee.

The government announced it was spending £400 million on keeping down the spiralling costs of the 2012 London Olympics. Tory MP Philip Davies said: 'We are going hundreds of millions further over budget to make sure we stay on budget. It is the most absurd, bonkers thing I have ever heard.'

Six car bombs went off in a busy market in Sadr City, a Baghdad slum and Shia stronghold, killing 160 and wounding 260 and sparking a backlash against Sunni neighbourhoods.

Former Russian spy Aleksandr Litvinenko died in a London hospital after apparently being poisoned. Hours earlier the arch-critic of Vladimir Putin said: 'The bastards got me. They won't get us all.'

Loyalist killer Michael Stone charged into the Stormont Assembly building, carrying a pistol and a knife and shouting: 'No surrender.' He was stopped and disarmed by two security officers. A key debate on power-sharing was halted. Stone was charged with several counts of attempted murder, with Gerry Adams and Martin McGuinness among his targets. His parole was revoked (see July 2000).

US State Department analyst Kendall Myers said that Britain's role as a bridge between America and Europe was 'disappearing before our eyes'. He exposed the myth of a mutually beneficial relationship between Blair and Bush, saying: 'It was a one-sided relationship that was entered into with open eyes . . . there was no payback, no sense of reciprocity.'

Gordon Brown revealed that his four-month-old son Fraser had cystic fibrosis.

'It's a fact that the very first achievement of this Labour government was to install a coin-operated tights machine.' – Labour MP Rosemary McKenna.

December

Blair announced a £25 billion programme to replace the submarine fleet carrying Trident nuclear missiles but pledged that the number of warheads would be reduced. Up to eighty Labour backbenchers threatened to rebel.

Blair said that immigrants must conform with British values and that their duty to integrate took precedence over cultural and religious practices.

Cherie Blair said that her husband always bought Christmas presents for herself and her mother, 'otherwise he's dead'.

Former Chilean dictator Augusto Pinochet, said to be responsible for the murder of at least 3,000 of his own people, died aged ninety-one. Lady Thatcher mourned her old friend and Falklands ally.

Five prostitutes were murdered in six weeks, their stripped bodies found near Ipswich. The 'Suffolk Ripper' case led to massive public sympathy and calls for a review of the prostitution laws. A fork-lift truck-driver was charged with the murders.

Blair became the first-ever Prime Minister to be questioned by police engaged in a criminal investigation. Officers quizzed him in No. 10 for two hours over why he had nominated for peerages people who had made secret loans to Labour. Blair told police that he had no knowledge of 'secret gifts' received by Labour, sparking a third police interview of Lord Levy. Blair gave Levy his full backing. It later emerged that Blair's chief of staff, Jonathan Powell, was to be grilled in the New Year after e-mails allegedly implicating him were uncovered.

Downing Street was accused of timing the police interview to coincide with the publication of Lord Stevens's report on Princess Diana's death in a failed bid to 'bury' bad news. The 832-page report ruled that there was no conspiracy to murder Diana. Princes William and Harry called for an end to conspiracy stories over the death of their mother. But Mohammed al-Fayed rejected the £3.6 million investigation as a 'cover-up'.

Former Defence Secretary Geoff Hoon was summonsed by a coroner over claims that he delayed supplying full body armour to British troops in Iraq. Hoon sent MoD officials instead. Coroner Andrew Walker described the delay as 'unforgivable and inexcusable'.

Trade and Industry Secretary Alistair Darling announced the closure of another 2,500 post offices.

Blair flew to Basra and told troops he would not cut and run in the fight for democracy. 'Our country is having to rediscover what it means to fight for what we believe in,' he said. He flew on to Jerusalem as Gaza erupted in Palestinian factional warfare.

An ICM poll put the Tories at their highest rating in fourteen years – up three points to 40 per cent, with Labour static on 32 per cent and the Liberal Democrats down four points to 18 per cent, their lowest since 1992.

A British soldier, Corporal Daniel James, was charged with treason and giving Iran secret information about the Afghanistan campaign. He was interpreter to Lieutenant General David Richards, head of the NATO security force in Afghanistan.

Official figures showed that more young people were out of work than when Labour came to power – 702,000 16–24-year-olds, 37,000 more than in May 2007, contradicting Blair's September claim.

The Archbishop of Canterbury, Dr Rowan Williams, claimed that

Christians in the Middle East were being put at risk by the government's 'short-sighted and ignorant' policy in Iraq.

The UN security council unanimously approved sanctions against Iran for refusing to suspend its uranium enrichment programme. Margaret Beckett said: 'Iran faces a choice between a route that allows it to develop a modern civil nuclear power programme or further defiance and the costs of isolation.'

A leaked report from Blair's Downing Street Strategy Unit warned that crime would increase for the first time in a decade and that the prison population would jump 25 per cent to 100,000. One factor was 'an increasing wealth gap . . . the very poorest have got poorer since 1997.' Blair's 'tough on crime, tough on the causes of crime' strategy had been undermined because Gordon Brown had frozen Home Office spending, including prison-building.

A Tory review of teaching history in schools left out Churchill and Thatcher in its list of Great Britons, but included Labour's Aneurin Bevan, founder of the NHS.

An Iraqi appeals court turned down Saddam Hussein's appeal, ruling he should be executed within thirty days.

More people took part in Boxing Day hunts than on any day in recent history, the meets attracting 300,000 people across the country.

British and US troops attacked and destroyed a Basra police

station believed to be a centre for organised crime and kidnappings, freeing 127 prisoners said to be on the brink of execution.

The Tories faced a Commons inquiry into claims that parliamentary dining rooms had been used to raise cash for fighting marginal seats at the next election.

Prescott was left in charge as the Blairs flew to Florida to holiday at the luxury home of Bee Gee Robin Gibb. Downing Street insisted that the family had paid its way, something denied by Gibb's wife Dwina, who said: 'It's just a friendly thing.' Lib Dem Norman Baker disagreed: 'It's shameless, it's greedy, it's grasping.'

Rock star Rod Stewart was awarded a CBE in the New Year Honours list. MI6 head John Scarlett received a knighthood, sparking claims he had been rewarded for taking responsibility for the 'dodgy dossier' on Saddam's phantom arsenal.

30th: Saddam Hussein was hanged at dawn. He went to his death calmly, watched on TV by an estimated one billion people. George W. Bush said: 'Bringing him to justice will not end the violence in Iraq but it is an important milestone on Iraq's course to become a democracy that can govern, sustain and defend itself.' Margaret Beckett said: 'I welcome the fact that Saddam Hussein has been tried by an Iraqi court for at least some of the appalling crimes he committed against the Iraqi people. He has now been held to account.' Sameer Redha, 23, of the Shia city Najaf said: 'I never saw my father. My mother said Saddam executed him. I had a terrible life because of Saddam. I will be able to enjoy life.' Rasha Oudeh, with Saddam's daughters Raghad and Rana as they watched the last moments on TV, said: 'They felt very proud as they saw their father facing his executioners so bravely, standing up.' Mobile phone video footage captured Saddam's executioners taunting him, and the trapdoor dropped halfway through his last prayer, enraging Sunnis. Car bombs killed more than eighty within hours of his execution.

'[Tony Blair] has had a brilliant year. I say that because of this simple, undeniable fact. He is still there. There he is, still in Downing Street. Despite the resurgent Tories, despite his own revolting party, despite Gordon, despite Iraq, despite cash for coronets, despite it all, the great survivor is still there. Any one of [them] . . . might have finished off a Prime Minister. He endured them all. Time and again, the Houdini of Downing Street escaped to live another day.' – Andrew Rawnsley, *Observer*.

2007

The bruising build-up to Blair's departure.

January

In his New Year message Tony Blair warned that Labour could only win a fourth term if it kept its core coalition together and continued his reforming agenda. 'This is the most difficult time for any government,' he said. 'Nine years into power, mid-term in a third term – Labour has never been in this position before.' But he insisted that the party could 'take heart since it is dominating the battle of ideas and will continue to do so provided it continues to be New Labour'.

Five-year-old Ellie Lawrenson was killed by her uncle's 'pit bull terrier-type' dog in St Helens, Merseyside, prompting calls for tightening of dangerous dogs legislation.

Parliamentary sleaze-buster Sir Philip Mawer declared that ministers with grace-and-favour residences should not claim accommodation allowances of up to £22,000 a year to fund second homes in London. Top beneficiaries were Blair, Gordon Brown, John Prescott, Jack Straw and Margaret Beckett. Overall, MPs claimed £86.7 million in expenses and office allowances, averaging £134,000 each on top of their £60,000 salaries.

Blair cut short his winter holiday in Florida for Ulster crisis talks after Sinn Fein warned that a special conference on its attitude to policing might not go ahead. The PM threatened to call off May elections for the Northern Ireland Assembly.

John Reid insisted that the New Labour policy of meeting the increased aspirations of families must continue after Blair otherwise the party would lose the next election. John Prescott said it was mistaken to portray Gordon Brown as Old Labour. A survey by deputy leadership contender John Cruddas found that two-thirds of voters had had no contact from Labour since the May 2005 general election.

Army wives battled to improve their 'squalid' barracks homes.

Both Brown and Prescott described the manner of Saddam Hussein's execution as 'deplorable'. Blair took ten days to comment, eventually saying: 'The crimes that Saddam committed do not excuse the manner of his execution but the manner of his execution does not excuse the crimes.' QC Philippe Sands said it was 'plausible' that Blair could face a UN war crimes tribunal.

Former Education Secretary Ruth Kelly enrolled her nine-year-old son in a £15,000-a-year prep school. The Communities Secretary was accused of hypocrisy but claimed that the boy had special needs. She said: 'Like any parent, my first thought was for my child.'

John Reid admitted that 27,500 files on crimes committed abroad had not been stored on the national police computer, including those of five murderers, twenty-five rapists and twenty-nine paedophiles. Police claimed that they had warned junior ministers of the fiasco three months earlier. Reid said he found it 'inexplicable' that the backlog had not been brought to his attention. A senior civil servant was suspended. The Prison Service revealed that two murderers had walked out of an open jail in Derbyshire. Reid also scrapped the Assets Recovery Agency after it emerged it had spent £60 million to retrieve just £8.3 million from criminals.

American warplanes struck suspected al-Qaida centres in Somalia. President Bush announced a surge of 21,500 more US troops to Iraq to purge Baghdad of Shia militias, and to kill Sunni and al-Qaida insurgents. Republican Senator Chuck Hagel said: 'This represents the most dangerous foreign policy blunder since Vietnam.' Royal Marines wiped out 100 Taliban fighters in an Afghan ambush.

Interest rates rose a quarter point to 5.25 per cent, the third hike in six months.

Saddam's half-brother and intelligence chief Barzan Ibrahim al-Tikriti was hanged for war crimes. The execution severed his head.

Blair endorsed a 'Big Brother' scheme to allow information on every British citizen to be shared by government departments. Shami Chakrabarti, director of Liberty, said: 'This half-baked proposal would allow an information free-for-all – ripe for disastrous errors and ripe for corruption and fraud.'

Downing Street advertised for a £50,000-a-year butler, it emerged, but the position has yet to be filled. The cost of running No. 10 trebled under Blair, up from £6 million to £17.8 million. Tony and Cherie got free British Airways upgrades worth £6,000 for their Miami holiday. A BA spokesman said: 'This is normal on busy flights.'

Gordon Brown, on a trip to India, urged *Big Brother* viewers to vote Jade Goody out after she and others in the household were seen bullying and making foul-mouthed and allegedly racist comments at Bollywood star Shilpa Shetty. The row sparked outrage in the sub-continent, shamed Britain abroad, threatened lucrative trade deals and led to a debate at home about racism and yobbishness. Shetty won the contest by a heavy margin.

Ruth Turner, one of Blair's closest aides, was arrested and grilled for several hours over claims that she suppressed evidence in the cash-for-peerages affair. She insisted she had done nothing wrong. Blair was again interviewed as a witness by police who, No. 10 claimed, insisted that their actions should be kept under wraps for six days. Before the news blackout was lifted police arrested Labour fund-raiser Lord Levy for a second time. He was released on bail.

Blair was forced to back down when Cabinet colleagues insisted that Catholic adoption agencies should not bar gay couples adopting children.

John Reid faced a storm when he told judges not to impose jail sentences, because the prisons were full. Two alleged paedophiles were released on bail as the judges rebelled against his guidelines. It was later claimed that ministers had known about hundreds of missing sex offenders three years ago.

Director of Public Prosecutions Sir Ken Macdonald rejected the concept of a 'war on terror'. He said: 'London is not a battlefield. Those innocents who were murdered on 7 July 2005 were not victims of war. And the men who killed them were not, as in their vanity they claim on their ludicrous videos, soldiers.'

Sinn Fein ended an 86-year boycott of policing in Northern Ireland as part of its bid to share power.

Britain's first super-casino was awarded to Manchester, not frontrunners Blackpool or the Millennium Dome. The winning bid was led by South African billionaire Sol Kerzner, reputed to have close links with New Labour.

Nine British Muslim suspects were arrested in Birmingham. Police claimed to have smashed an Al-Qaida plot to kidnap a British Muslim soldier and behead him on camera. Five were later charged with terrorist offences.

'Provided we go to New New Labour and don't retreat from New Labour, we will come through this.' – Tony Blair.

'The Blair premiership is a classic illustration of the potential for good intentions to turn to dust.' – Sacked Home Secretary Charles Clarke.

'Leave a message after the high moral tone.' – Downing Street answering machine, according to a Whitehall joke.

'I'm going to finish what I started.' – Tony Blair, insisting that the past eighteen months had been 'our most radical, our most bold'.

February

Frank Field urged that all immigrants should speak English before arrival.

Conservative leader David Cameron urged the PM to take a 'reality check' and quit in the national interest. An anonymous aide to a Blairite minister said: 'No. 10 now resembles Hitler's bunker. You have conversations with them and come away with the impression that they are living on a different planet to the rest of us.'

Smokers will risk £200 fines if they light up in the wrong place when the work and public place ban comes into effect on 1 July, health officials announced.

Former Labour MP Fiona Jones, one of 'Blair's Babes', died aged forty-nine. Her husband Chris blamed the 'drink culture' at the Commons.

Archbishop of York Dr John Sentamu warned that Britain was turning into an Idi Amin-style police state.

Dramatic tapes were released highlighting the death in 2003 of Lance Corporal of Horse Matty Hull in 'friendly fire' by American pilots, one of whom was heard saying: 'We're in jail, dude.'

Seven letter bombs exploded in offices ranging from the DVLA in Swansea to business outsourcing company Capita's HQ in London, injuring a dozen staff. All the offices were connected to either driving or DNA testing.

An outbreak of bird flu at Bernard Matthews's farm in Suffolk led to the slaughter of 180,000 turkeys and a national panic. Chief scientific officer Sir David King voiced concern that wild birds could be contaminated with the H5N1 virus.

A million people signed a petition, posted on the Downing Street website, opposed to nationwide road congestion charges. The Downing Street aide who thought up the e-petition, described by one minister as a 'prat', was revealed to be Benjamin Wegg-Prosser, a former advisor to Peter Mandelson. Tony Blair said: 'It's a sign of just how fast politics has changed in the last decade that, while I was once criticised for being a control freak, I now find myself under attack for allowing dissenting views on my own website.'

David Cameron narrowly escaped being expelled from Eton for smoking cannabis and continued toking at Oxford, it was revealed. The Tory leader refused to comment.

More than eighty people were killed by car bombers in Baghdad markets on the first anniversary of the destruction of the Al-

Askari shrine. The carnage took the civilian death toll in Iraq to at least 33,937 in twelve months.

Tony Blair announced the withdrawal of 1,600 British troops from Iraq by the summer. He later said: 'I don't think we should be apologising, because we're not causing the terrorism.' A former ambassador to Iraq, Sir Jeremy Greenstock, claimed that Blair had 'taken his eye off the ball' during the post-war period. He said: 'There was a vacuum from the beginning in which looters, saboteurs, the criminals, the insurgents, moved very quickly.' Prince Harry was told he would be going to the Iraq front line with his Blues and Royals comrades.

A UNICEF report ranked British children as the worst off in the world's twenty-one richest nations. Another report found that only two million mothers stay at home to look after their offspring.

Three black teenagers were shot dead in south London over a two-week period, sparking claims that youth crime and gun culture were out of control. Blair declared that the age threshold for a mandatory five-year sentence for carrying guns would be lowered from twenty-one to seventeen.

Attorney-General Lord Goldsmith was forced to admit to an affair with a prominent female lawyer.

Blair aide Ruth Turner was questioned again by police probing the cash-for-peerages affair.

Ministers admitted that 25 per cent of British pensioners were facing poverty, compared to a European average of 18 per cent.

Michael Meacher announced that he was standing for the Labour leadership – only four colleagues turned up in support.

On a visit to Manchester David Cameron was pictured with a hoodie pretending to shoot him in the back of the head.

'Allowing Gordon Brown into No. 10 would be like letting Mrs Rochester out of the attic.' – Frank Field.

'I like to be liked . . . I have tried to do my best over the last ten years.' – Tony Blair on the *Today* programme.

'Mr Spock without the human bits.' – Unnamed shadow Cabinet member on Gordon Brown.

'He's like a songwriter who's eternally ripping off someone else's song and just changing the odd line a little.' – Oasis star Noel Gallagher on David Cameron.

'Smoothies are wonderful for drinking but not so good for running the country.' – Welsh First Minister Rhodri Morgan on David Cameron.

March
The BBC was gagged from reporting a fresh angle on the cash-for-peerages scandal after Attorney-General Lord Goldsmith successfully applied for an injunction. It centred on an e-mail by

Ruth Turner in which she claimed Lord Levy had tried to bully her into adapting her evidence to the police inquiry. The injunction against publication of the 'killer e-mail' was lifted after an intervention by No. 10. Levy claimed he was being smeared. His friend Sir Alan Sugar claimed he was being made a scapegoat by Blair: 'With friends like him you don't need enemies.'

Top White House aide Lewis 'Scooter' Libby was found guilty of four counts of perjury over the leaking of the identity of a CIA agent whose husband opposed the Iraq War.

Tony Blair admitted his regret that his lengthy departure had created 'uncertainty' across his administration. In another interview he predicted that voters who deserted Labour over Iraq would flock back when he quit: 'When I go, then it goes with me.'

David Cameron vowed to support marriage with tax breaks, claiming that children from single-parent families did worse at school and were more likely to fall into crime. The Tory lead over Labour doubled to 8 per cent, according to a Populus poll.

Sir Menzies Campbell set out his conditions for a Lib Dem coalition with a Brown-led Labour government, including scrapping ID cards, means-testing for pensioner benefits and council tax.

MPs voted for a wholly elected House of Lords, defying the 50-50 preference of Blair and Jack Straw. Lib Dem David Heath said:

'I do hope that there isn't now a queue of noble Lords asking for a refund.'

David Cameron sacked homeland security spokesman Patrick Mercer after he appeared to suggest that being called a 'black bastard' was part of army life for ethnic minorities.

Ian Paisley came under intense pressure to enter a power-sharing agreement with Sinn Fein after his party made gains in the Northern Ireland Assembly elections. The DUP won 30 per cent of first-preference votes, Sin Fein 26 per cent, the SDLP 14 per cent, the UUP 15 per cent and the Alliance party 5 per cent. In a joint statement Blair and Irish premier Bertie Ahern said: 'The message of the electorate is clear: after so many years of frustration and disappointment, they want Northern Ireland to move to build a better future together through the devolved institutions.'

Ninety-five Labour MPs rebelled against Blair's plan for a £20 billion upgrade of Trident. He was saved by the Tories.

A coroner ruled that British soldier Matty Hull had been unlawfully killed by American airmen (see February 2007). Washington said they would not face prosecution. The cost to Britain of fighting the Iraq war and the subsequent occupation topped £5 billion. An Australian academic report estimated the overall death toll at one million, compared with earlier studies ranging from 60,000 to 650,000. British military deaths had reached 134 since 2003 while American losses had reached 3,218 dead and 23,417 wounded. The Pentagon was rocked by claims of appalling conditions in military hospitals.

Blair did an 'Am I bovvered?' double act with comedienne Catherine Tate for Comic Relief. She said afterwards: 'He is one of the finest comic actors of his generation.'

Lord Turnbull, former head of the civil service, accused Gordon Brown of 'Stalinist ruthlessness' and of treating colleagues with 'utter contempt'. A new poll suggested that Brown was trailing David Cameron by 15 per cent. Cameron said that Brown combined the 'tendencies of Stalin and the poll ratings of Michael Foot'.

Brown delivered his eleventh Budget: a 2p cut in the basic rate of income tax from April 2008, abolition of the bottom 10p rate for low earners, rises in national insurance, a 2p cut in corporation tax, road tax for gas-guzzlers almost doubled to £400, 11p on cigarettes, 1p on a pint, £1 billion more for schools, more help for victims of wound-up pensions. Brown's opinion poll rating slumped after a lukewarm public response.

Iran seized fifteen British service personnel on the disputed Shatt al-Arab waterway, sparking fears that they would be held as hostages in the tense stand-off over the Iranian nuclear programme. Iran claimed the British vessel was in its territorial waters, a claim vehemently denied by Britain. The prisoners were paraded on TV and forced to apologise for their actions. Blair expressed his 'disgust' and vowed that there would be no deals with the captors.

Ian Paisley and Gerry Adams agreed to share power in a restored Northern Ireland Assembly, in a deal which Northern Ireland Secretary Peter Hain described as 'really, really momentous'. Paisley said: 'We must not allow our loathing of the horrors and tragedies of the past to become a barrier to creating a better and more stable future for our children.' Adams said: 'The relationships between the people of this island have been marred by centuries of hurt and tragedy . . . We have created the potential to build a new, harmonious and equitable relationship.'

Documents released under the Freedom of Information Act revealed that officials warned Gordon Brown ahead of his first 1997 Budget that tax changes would cost occupational and private pensions up to £75 billion. He ignored them and the revelations led to further questions about his fitness to replace Blair.

April

After a tense thirteen-day stand-off, Iranian President Mahmoud Ahmadinejad released the fifteen captured naval personnel. In a live broadcast screened globally he denounced Britain and America but set free the group to mark the birthday of Muhammad and the 'passing of Christ'. Opinion was divided over whether it was a triumph for British diplomacy and Tony Blair's tough stance, or a total humiliation. Either way, Iran won a major propaganda victory. Blair said: 'We have done this without any deal, without any negotiation, without any side agreement of any nature whatsoever.' Eyebrows were raised when two of the fifteen were permitted to sell their stories to the newspapers. An outcry over 'cash for cowardice' prevented the others following suit. Defence Secretary Des Browne took responsibility – but also blamed naval chiefs. He made a qualified apology and kept his job.

'The Iranian farce marks a new low point, a propaganda disaster for us across the world.' – Former Tory Defence Secretary Michael Heseltine.

A BPIX poll showed that a majority of the public had lost faith in Blair and his government, including Gordon Brown, and that they believed Britain was now a less pleasant, more dangerous place to live than in 1997.

Scottish Nationalist MP Angus MacNeil, who triggered the cash-for-peerages inquiry, was forced to apologise to his family after it was revealed he had enjoyed a 'drunken romp' with two teenage girls in 2005, only weeks before his wife gave birth.

Blair told the black community to do more to eliminate knife crime, saying: 'We won't stop this by pretending it isn't young black kids doing it.' Brown met President George Bush for their first face-to-face chat. Labour, hit by a shortage of candidates, decided to contest just 60 per cent of the seats in the upcoming local government elections. Lord Bruce-Lockhart, chairman of the Local Government Association, said: 'It shows a worrying lack of belief in local democracy.'

It emerged that Brown had cost the country £2 billion in the late 1990s by selling gold reserves at the bottom of the market, disregarding Bank of England advice.

The Register of Members' Interests revealed that over the last year William Hague raked in more than £1 million from writing and public speaking, while David Blunkett trousered £580,000 and George Galloway made £305,000.

Inflation rose 0.3 points to 3.1 per cent, the highest for fifteen years.

At least 183 people were killed in four bombings in Baghdad, the city's highest death toll in a single day.

Police recommended that Lord Levy and Ruth Turner should be charged over the cash-for-honours affair. A Crown Prosecution Service decision was expected in three months.

The wealth of Britain's 1,000 richest people had more than trebled since Blair came to power, according to the *Sunday Times* Rich List.

Twelve British soldiers were killed in Iraq during April, the highest monthly toll since the war. Army chiefs confirmed that Prince Harry would be deployed in Basra despite threats from insurgents to kill or kidnap him.

Five British Muslims were sentenced to life for plotting a terror blitz using fertiliser bombs at the Bluewater shopping centre in Kent, the London nightclub Ministry of Sound and other targets. MI5 were accused of incompetence after the trial revealed that the massive surveillance operation which resulted in the convictions featured two 7/7 suicide bombers over a year before the attacks on London. John Reid refused a public inquiry into the blunder, saying: 'It would divert the energies and efforts of so many who are already stretched in countering the threat.'

'I think we're moving away from this period when, if you like, celebrity matters, where people have become famous for being famous. People are moving away from that to what lies behind the character and the personality.' – Gordon Brown.

'I did maths at school and for one year at university but I don't think I was ever very good at it.' – Gordon Brown.

'I think when I go, obviously a lot of the static and unpopularity that attaches itself to any Prime Minister over ten years goes with me.' – Tony Blair.

'I know a great deal more about the world today than I ever did in government.' – John Major.

May

On the tenth anniversary of his taking power, Blair finally endorsed Gordon Brown as his successor, telling a Scottish audience: 'Within the next few weeks I won't be Prime Minister of this country. In all probability a Scot will become Prime Minister of the United Kingdom. That's someone who has built one of the strongest economies in the world and who I've always said will make a great Prime Minister.' Downing Street denied reports that Blair was planning to stand down as an MP before the summer, sparking a by-election. Charles Clarke declared he would not be standing against Brown because there was 'no appetite' in the party for a contest.

In English local government elections Labour lost nearly 500 seats, while the Tories gained more than 875 after inflicting defeat on both Labour and the Lib Dems. Labour won some in the northern regions, deepening the political north/south divide. In Scotland the SNP became the biggest party in the Edinburgh Parliament, overturning fifty years of Labour dominance north of the border, but the contest was marred by up to 100,000 spoilt ballot papers. Further Labour losses left Wales heading for a coalition government. Tony Blair said the results were 'a perfectly good springboard to go on and win the next election'. David Cameron said: 'We are now the party of the whole country.' Sir Menzies Campbell said: 'Ours is a national party of local government.'

'The man is so pleased with himself, he'd drink his own bathwater.' – Unnamed Scottish voter on SNP leader Alex Salmond, quoted in the *Daily Telegraph*.

John Reid announced that he would be resigning from the Cabinet when Blair left in June. He said: 'I need to recharge my batteries,' and pointed out he had had nine government jobs in ten years. Finally ruling himself out of the leadership contest, he endorsed Gordon Brown, saying that there was 'no stomach' in the party for a contest. But his move prompted speculation that he could not face working with his 'oldest political acquaintance'.

Devolution was finally resumed at Stormont with First Minister

Ian Paisley and Martin McGuinness heading a power-sharing Northern Ireland Assembly. Paisley said: 'We have come to a time of peace, a time when hate will no longer rule.' McGuinness said: 'We must look to the future. The road will have many twists and turns.' Onlooker Blair said: 'People felt that it could not be done. Yet in the end it was, and this holds a lesson for conflict everywhere.' And his predecessor, John Major, said: 'There will be setbacks. But will this come apart at the seams? I don't think so.'

'I should have taken a lesson from you and kept going until I was eighty.' – Tony Blair to Ian Paisley.

David Cameron claimed that the government would be paralysed for seven weeks during the Blair–Brown handover as no Cabinet ministers would know what their future held, adding: 'This is the government of the living dead.'

10th: *Blair announces resignation*
Tony Blair announced at Trimdon Labour club in his Sedgefield constituency that he would hand his resignation to the Queen on 27 June, saying: 'I have been Prime Minister of this country for just over ten years . . . that is long enough for me, but more especially for the country.' In an emotional statement he apologised for the times he had fallen short of expectations, but insisted: 'Hand on heart, I did what I thought was right.' He said he had been right to remove Saddam Hussein but admitted: 'The blowback has been fierce, unrelenting and costly. For many it can't be worth it. For me, I think we must see it through. The terrorists who threaten us here and around the world will never give up if we

give up. It is a test of wills and we can't fail.' He said that Britain was now no longer a follower but a leader, adding: 'It is a country comfortable in the twenty-first century, at home in its own skin, able not just to be proud of its past, but also confident of its future.' Choking back a tear he told the country: 'Good luck.' He was played out by the New Labour anthem 'Things Can Only Get Better'.

John Prescott bowed out more quietly, saying that holding the post of deputy premier for a decade had been 'a source of great pride'.

Gordon Brown launched his premiership bid by promising a break with the Blair era, the ditching of spin and the culture of celebrity and a government 'humble enough to know its place'. He said that while Blair had led the country with 'distinction, courage, passion and insight', he now offered 'a new leadership for a new time'. The launch was marred by a teleprompter screen which obscured his face and by his being inadvertently locked out of one venue.

'I am absolutely delighted to give my full support to Gordon as the next leader of the Labour Party and as Prime Minister and to endorse him fully. I think he has got what it takes to lead . . . with distinction. He is an extraordinary and rare talent and it's a tremendous thing if it's put at the service of the nation, as it now can be.' – Tony Blair.

*

Prince Harry was told that he would not be going to Iraq to join his unit. Army head Sir Richard Dannatt ruled that specific threats made it too dangerous for the 22-year-old and his comrades.

Brown secured 308 nominations from Labour MPs, ensuring that he would become leader with no contest. His only challenger, left-wing MP John McDonnell, conceded defeat and withdrew.

Prescott took his last Prime Minister's Question Time, later saying: 'I know they call me thick and dumbo but I have thought about policy as much as anybody in the Cabinet.' Commons sketch-writer Quentin Letts commented: 'He's been a gargoyle on the guttering of government.'

Cameron provoked Tory outrage when he dumped the party's commitment to grammar schools. He said: 'We will never be taken seriously by parents and convince them we are on their side and share their aspirations if we splash around in the shallow end of the education debate.' Europe spokesman Graham Brady resigned in protest. Later Cameron was forced to perform a U-turn, accepting that some new grammars could be built. Tory disquiet escalated when shadow Chancellor George Osborne suggested that Cameron would continue public service reforms and was the 'true heir' to Blair. Traditional Tories grew apoplectic when Andy Coulson, former *News of the World* editor, was appointed the party's head of communications. An Ipsos MORI poll showed a slump in Conservative support from 42 to 37 per cent.

Tony Blair would declare himself a Roman Catholic after leaving Downing Street, priest and confidant Father Michael Seed predicted. Blair made a farewell visit to Washington. He insisted that he would make the same decision to remove Saddam today. 'I believe that September 11th was an attack on all of us,' he told broadcasters. President Bush admitted that he could be partly to blame for Blair's premature exit.

Alex Salmond made history as the first Nationalist to be elected Scotland's First Minister after a 49-46 vote in the Holyrood Parliament. He stressed compromise and concession, hoping that good governance rather than confrontation would boost the independence cause.

Blair is to have a bomb-proof, custom-made Land Rover Discovery, it was revealed, the most expensive vehicle ever delivered to an ex-PM. It was unclear whether he would pick up a share of the £150,000 cost. Cherie reportedly put pressure on him to prepare lucrative lecture tours to help finance mortgages allegedly totalling £5 million spread across five properties, costing £20,000 a month. An anonymous 'insider' said: 'Cherie is incredibly stressed, grumpy and bad-tempered, and . . . she has been snapping at everyone. Tony just seems bereft now he is coming to the end of the road. He is very low. In truth, Tony is in total denial about the fact that he is about to give up his status as the world's second most powerful man and all the trappings that go with it.'

Mortar bombs rocked Blair's surprise farewell visit to Iraq. Shortly before he arrived the British embassy compound in Baghdad was hit, and later the same day the Army HQ in Basra was attacked minutes after he left. Officials played down any suggestion that insurgents had mounted an assassination attempt on the PM.

Blair said: 'There are mortar attacks and terrorist attacks happening every day, that's the reality. The question is, what are we going to do in the face of these attacks? The answer is, we don't give in to them.'

Former premier Sir John Major claimed that Blair was 'in the middle of the longest farewell since Dame Nellie Melba quit the stage'. Joe Haines, Harold Wilson's former press supremo, urged Brown not to ape the more charismatic Blair, saying: 'It wouldn't ring true, like Dawn French sashaying down the catwalk following Kate Moss.'

Communities Secretary Ruth Kelly was forced to delay the introduction of expensive home information packs just ten days before their deadline following a legal challenge and a shortage of assessors. She vowed they would be introduced by the end of the year. Environment Secretary David Miliband warned of hefty fines if householders did not pay extra for domestic rubbish collection.

Blair and Reid unveiled new anti-terror legislation to give police sweeping powers to stop and question anyone, anywhere, anytime, sparking a civil liberties outcry and a Cabinet split.

Blair asked Alastair Campbell to tone down his (the PM's) foul-mouthed tirades in the former press supremo's upcoming diaries. Cherie Blair was reported to have seethed at the 'fantastically indiscreet' entries in the original draft of the diaries, particularly intimate episodes involving her children.

The Blairs embarked on a 'vanity' tour of Africa, landing first in Libya to meet Colonel Gaddafi before going on to Sierra Leone and South Africa. Critics focused on the presence of a writer and two photographers from the US glossy magazine *Men's Vogue* on the taxpayer-funded trip. Tory frontbencher Chris Grayling said: 'He seems more concerned about how he looks in *Vogue* than tackling real issues at home. It's time we brought an end to this farce.' The Tories also claimed, as Blair landed in Johannesburg, that the bill to the taxpayer for the farewell tour had already topped £1 million in transportation.

'We look forward to welcoming a young man like you into the club of retired Presidents. I need to warn you that some of us only become active after stepping down from public affairs.' – Nelson Mandela to Blair.

Five Britons, an IT expert and four bodyguards, were kidnapped by eighty heavily armed men wearing police and commando uniforms who burst into the Iraqi finance ministry in Baghdad. The Shia Mahdi Army claimed responsibility, saying that the seizures were in revenge for the death of its leader in a Basra operation involving UK troops.

Brown warned the six Labour deputy leadership contenders that there would be no shift to the left and his administration would continue to occupy the middle ground. His move came after Education Secretary Alan Johnson called for private school-teachers to be sent to work in the state sector, Northern Ireland Secretary Peter Hain demanded a crackdown on City bonuses, International Development Secretary Hilary Benn and party chairman Hazel Blears both urged a boost in trade union power, Justice Minister Harriet Harman advocated wealth confiscation to aid the poor, and backbencher Jon Cruddas favoured an amnesty for illegal immigrants.

'If you go down, I'm going down with you. I couldn't face the paperwork, sir.' – Armed protection officer briefing John Reid on what would happen if he was shot.

'I fear you might be right. This is a British tradition that must not be lost. If I were running for office again, I'd make it a major part of any platform.' – Tony Blair, after being told it was impossible to get a decent cup of tea in London.

'He is our saviour. Tony Blair is our redeemer.' – Kalie Bangura of Mahera, Sierra Leone, on learning that the outgoing PM would visit her country, previously ravaged by civil war.

June

John Prescott was admitted to hospital suffering from pneumonia two days after his sixty-ninth birthday.

A bruising confrontation with Russia's Vladimir Putin in Heiligendamm soured Tony Blair's last G8 summit. The PM raised the murder of former spy Aleksandr Litvinenko, the treatment of British companies in Russia and Putin's threat to train missiles on Europe. After a frosty response Blair predicted a lengthy period of deep freeze in relations with the West.

A dossier compiled by the Council of Europe found that Britain did help the CIA fly terror suspects to secret torture centres. The report said that two secret prisons in Poland and Romania took inmates with the logistical support of UK civilian and military airports. The Council said that the CIA, with British help, had been pursuing a war on terror with no rules.

Saudi prince Bandar bin Sultan was alleged to have received £1 billion over ten years in payments to help secure a BAE Systems arms deal and to have met Blair in July 2006 at the height of a Serious Fraud Office investigation.

Lakshmi Mittal, Britain's richest man and one of Labour's biggest donors, was accused by unions of exploiting 'slave labour' conditions in his Kazakh mines when it emerged that explosions had killed more than fifty workers since 2004.

Blair savaged the media, saying that the 24-hour news agenda could 'overwhelm' his successor. He said: 'The fear of missing out means today's media, more than ever before, hunts in a pack. In these modes it is like a feral beast, just tearing people and reputations to bits.'

The government's Commission on Integration and Cohesion reported that racial tensions were 'bubbling under the surface' in many parts of the country. Communities Secretary Ruth Kelly said: 'This is a wake-up call.'

Knighthoods went to fatwa author Salman Rushdie, cricketer Ian Botham and Barry Humphries, a.k.a. Dame Edna Everage, in the

Queen's Birthday Honours list. KGB defector Oleg Gordievsky was rewarded with a CMG.

Blair was forced to deny claims by former aides that he knew that the USA had no follow-up strategy to the invasion of Iraq and the toppling of Saddam. He insisted that the real turning point came in August 2003 when the UN building in Baghdad was blown up by a truck bomb. He also told the Commons Liaison Committee that he never really believed in an elected House of Lords, having always favoured an appointed second chamber. Tory MP Edward Leigh told him: 'On your political tombstone will be one word – Iraq.' Blair replied: 'I don't write what's on my tombstone.'

Barry Cox, a long-time Blair friend, claimed in a Channel 4 documentary that Cherie was incensed by Gordon Brown's behaviour towards her husband. The programme also claimed that No. 10 staff felt that Tony and Gordon were like 'children in a dysfunctional relationship'; that Blair regretted agreeing a compromise with Brown over foundation hospitals; that Treasury officials believed it was the 'kiss of death' to co-operate with No. 10; and that then party chairman Alan Milburn regarded Blair's decision to pre-announce his resignation as 'mad'.

Joseph Corre, boss of the Agent Provocateur lingerie firm, rejected his MBE because Blair was, he claimed, 'morally corrupt'.

Former Lib Dem leader Paddy Ashdown turned down an offer by Gordon Brown of an unspecified place in the Cabinet. Current leader Sir Menzies Campbell, after a meeting with

Brown, ordered that no Lib Dem member should accept any post in the Brown administration.

Asked why he did not wear body armour during his recent visit to Baghdad, Blair replied that he was more likely to be assassinated on walkabout in the streets of Birmingham. He also revealed that he had worn the same pair of 'lucky' shoes at every PM's Question Time over the last ten years.

On President Bush and the charge that he embraced the American right wing, he said: 'I'm not going to apologise for having a relationship with someone I've found to be straight and true to his word. I wouldn't agree with most American politicians on the death penalty. I think that gay rights are a big deal. I introduced a law banning handguns. But I can't understand how removing the Taliban and Saddam Hussein, who stood for the most repressive reactionary values imaginable, I can't see how that's right-wing. And when people say to me: "Bush is a bog standard ultra-right-wing Republican," I say: "Well, who's got a black woman as Secretary of State?"'

Lord Goldsmith resigned as Attorney General just days before he was expected to be sacked when Brown became PM. He said he had been 'immensely privileged' to have served in the Blair government but had 'wanted to go for some time'. His departure increased speculation that Brown was to give independence to the Crown Prosecution Service, thereby distancing his government from a decision on whether or not to prosecute over the cash-for-peerages affair.

Blair chaired his last full Cabinet. Brown told him: 'Whatever we achieve in the future will be because we are standing on your shoulders.'

Brown reportedly used his veto to stop Blair backing down at the latter's last Euro-summit in Brussels. Blair claimed he had got all he wanted out of the negotiations on a new charter to replace the stalled single constitution, including opt-outs on human rights, foreign policy and taxation.

Blair's meeting with Pope Benedict XVI concluded after twenty-five uneasy minutes, during which the Pontiff criticised him over Iraq, the Middle East, same-sex marriages, abortion and stem cell research on human embryos. The visit was nevertheless seen as another step towards Blair becoming a fully fledged Roman Catholic.

With a brief handshake, Brown replaced Blair as Labour leader at a Manchester special conference. Brown promised to 'heed the call of change' and added: 'The party I lead must have more than a set of policies – it must have a soul.' Blair said of him: 'I know from his character that he will give of his best in the service of our country and I know from his record as Chancellor that his best is as good as it gets.' Harriet Harman beat Alan Johnson by a 1 per cent margin in the deputy leadership contest. Brown immediately appointed her party chairman – rather than deputy PM – and put Transport Secretary Douglas Alexander in charge of election strategy, sparking speculation that Brown could go to the polls as early as spring 2008. Harman delivered her first blunder within twenty-four hours by saying that the Iraq war was 'wrong' and then claiming she had been misquoted.

After a whip-round, ministers, MPs and peers presented Blair with a steel-string acoustic guitar. He told the parliamentary party: 'Go out there and be proud of our achievements.' John Prescott was presented with a tantalus decanter set. The following morning *Terminator* star and California governor Arnold Schwarzenegger presented Blair with yet another guitar.

Irish premier Bertie Ahern, recently re-elected, announced a £5 million Dublin-funded Tony Blair Chair of Irish Studies at Liverpool University, saying: 'It is a fitting way to mark his immense and historic contribution in helping bring peace to Northern Ireland.'

Former shadow Northern Ireland Secretary Quentin Davies dramatically defected to Labour in a deal brokered personally by Brown. Davies told David Cameron in his resignation letter: 'Although you have many positive qualities, you have three – superficiality, unreliability and an apparent lack of any clear convictions – which in my view ought to exclude you from the position of national leadership.' Lord Tebbit said: 'This defection will raise the average standard of members on the Conservative side and lower it on the Labour side.'

On the eve of his final bow as PM, it emerged that Blair would stand down as MP for Sedgefield – forcing a by-election – to take up an expenses-only post as special international envoy for the Middle East. The appointment was confirmed by the Quartet of the USA, the UN, the EU and Russia after two days of discussions. In Palestine Hamas spokesman Fawzi Barhoom said: 'Tony Blair has acted as a terrorist in many Arab and Muslim states such as Iraq, Afghanistan and Somalia.'

'Can I congratulate you on the remarkable achievement of surviving ten years at the Treasury – even if it is twice as long as you wanted.' – Tory spokesman George Osborne to Gordon Brown at the latter's last Treasury Question Time.

'Blair was more of a tragic than a comic figure. Brown has more comic potential because he's perceived as being so serious.' – TV impressionist Rory Bremner.

27th: Brown replaces Blair as PM

Cherie Blair, leaving Downing Street for the last time, told media doorsteppers: 'Bye, I don't think we'll miss you.' She and all four children took their seats in the gallery to watch her husband's last Prime Minister's Question Time. He began sombrely, offering his condolences to the last three British service casualties in Iraq and praised the 'courage, dedication and commitment' of the armed forces. He added: 'I know that there are those who think that they face these dangers in vain. I do not, and I never will.' He gave the conventional recital of his appointments, adding to laughter: 'I will have no further meetings today. Or any other day.' Blair rattled through his government's achievement on public services, Northern Ireland and education. The event threatened to turn into a mutual admiration society as David Cameron, Sir Menzies Campbell and the Reverend Ian Paisley thanked him for his 'courtesy', a compliment he reciprocated. Blair told outspoken anti-European Sir Nicholas Winterton: '*Au revoir, auf Wiedersehen* and *arrivederci*' and made a laboured joke about picking up his P45. So far so predictable. But after thirty minutes the House was overcome with a tsunami of emotion, with all sides standing to applaud. The public gallery followed suit and as MPs poured out of the chamber some, not all of them ultra-Blairite loyalists, were sobbing.

'Even though he is like nailing jelly to a wall, he is an extraordinary political performer. We won't see his like again for a long time. In the Conservative Party we are pretty thankful for that.' – Former Tory leader William Hague.

Blair, after a glass of champagne with No. 10 staff, went to Buckingham Palace to give the Queen his formal resignation. He emerged just before Gordon Brown arrived to accept the premiership. He and Cherie then took the train to Sedgefield to announce his resignation as MP. Both carried their own bags.

Blair's last words as PM in the Commons chamber had been: 'I wish everyone, friend and foe, well. And that is that. The end.'

The verdict

The real verdict on the Blair decade will be up to the historian, but that has not stopped others rushing to judgement. Unsurprisingly, opinion has been deeply divided on his record and his legacy.

For

'Blair has told friends he will embark on a mission to save the world from global warming. It is impossible not to admire the chutzpah and optimism of Tony Blair as, amid all the failures and disappointments, he struggles to find one more epic role – up like Sylvester Stallone for just one more Rocky.' – Jackie Ashley, *Guardian*, 12 February 2007.

'A man of enormous drive and vision, who has been determined to use his time in power to make a difference and [who] has brought about a lot of change for the better.' – Alastair Campbell, *Evening Standard*, 8 March 2007.

'What a great bloke! He has that fine, admirable schoolboy style.' Art Garfunkel, BBC Radio 2, 18 February 2007.

'What Blair has done is restore Britain to the status of a world power. It may be a world power lite, but it is a world power.' – Senior member of the Bush administration, *Newsweek*, 19 February 2007.

'He appears as a really easy-going guy, a nice guy to get along with. In some ways that's true. Co-existing with that is someone who is very ambitious, very ruthless . . .' Lord Wilson of Dinton, Cabinet Secretary 1998–2002, *Times*, 20 February 2007.

*

On Blair's Good Friday peace agreement and the subsequent peace process:

'I don't have any doubt whatsoever that if Tony Blair had not effectively laid it on the line to the leadership of the Ulster Unionist Party in particular that he wanted it by Good Friday 1998, then if he had not done that with the support of the Taoiseach the entire project would have collapsed.

'Where did his intellectual and emotional engagement in the process come from? It probably came from knowing and understanding that this was a conflict that had gone on for, at that stage, over twenty-five years. What powered him in all this? Was it a desire to be the first British Prime Minister in history to make an important contribution? It didn't really matter. What mattered was whether or not we were dealing with someone who made an impression on us. Someone who . . . was challenging the Thatcher mentality that the enemy was the republicans, the enemy was the IRA, that they had to be defeated at all costs. I think it was his willingness to do that which made an impression on us.' – Sinn Fein's Martin McGuinness, 14 March 2007.

'[Blair's] open-mindedness helped. John Major was another person who was very committed to trying to get progress in Northern Ireland. John was handicapped by the fact that his government had baggage, starting with the 1985 Anglo-Irish Agreement. Blair came in free of all that baggage. That was refreshing.

'You might say that while we didn't appreciate it at the time, here is a textbook example of the Blair soft government technique. Coming in, grabbing a particular issue, working on it himself in an informal way rather than through the normal official channels. In 1998 it worked and at other times it worked. Latterly this has become seen as a problem. But in 1998 this was novel and effective.' – Former Ulster Unionist leader Lord Trimble, 14 March 2007.

'He threw himself at it, for year after tortuous year, through all the cycles of stalemate, negotiation and breakthrough . . . He has displayed courage, ingenuity and persistence. He breathed new life into the peace process and then sustained it for all those exhausting years. In the tireless effort he has devoted to getting a settlement in Northern Ireland, Mr Blair has showcased his best qualities: his negotiating skills, his flair for creative ambiguity, a certain degree of deviousness, his capacity to take risks, and sheer effort of will.' – Andrew Rawnsley, *Observer*, 1 April 2007.

*

'He has transformed both his party and his opponents . . . Labour went from being a party that had been four-time losers into one that was three-time winners. The Tories have not been able to beat him and now feel compelled to copy him.

'His personal appeal has withered, but there is no sense that his governing ideal has been rejected. Both Gordon Brown and David Cameron are subscribers to the Blairology of economic efficiency combined with social justice and reformed public services. He has moved the centre of gravity of British politics and it has shifted to a more progressive place.

'Some Prime Ministers merely preside over their time. Better Prime Ministers change their time. When Tony Blair's portrait goes up on the staircase wall at No. 10, he will leave office with a good claim to belong to that select company of Prime Ministers who change the future.' – Andrew Rawnsley, *Observer*, 9 April 2007.

'Britain is better off after a decade with Tony Blair in charge of the most successful progressive government since Attlee. Wealth has been created and been distributed. That is what Labour governments have always hoped to do. It has happened without a brake on global competitiveness. That is what New Labour hoped to do: build a vibrant market economy with a generous welfare state; economic freedom and social protection. That is Blairism.' – Editorial, *Observer*, 29 April 2007.

'Ten years in office is pretty good going in itself. Have we become so mean-spirited that we cannot even applaud that achievement? To survive ten years in No. 10 is an extraordinarily difficult feat, particularly under the constant media scrutiny that

The verdict

Prime Ministers today have to face. To do so while raising a young family is almost superhuman.' – Alice Miles, *Times*, 9 May 2007.

'There are two issues I will be eternally grateful to Blair for. One is Ireland. If you had told me ten years ago I would have lived to see Gerry Adams sit down with Ian Paisley and talk, I wouldn't have believed you. The second thing is Africa. It was nowhere on the agenda before. Has the policy been successful? Yes. It has been heart-pounding.' – Bob Geldof, 10 May 2007.

'I think Tony Blair will go down in history as a great Prime Minister because, although his failure to change much domestically matters a lot now, it won't in forty or fifty years' time. People don't tend to judge Prime Ministers on obscure statistics. What they remember are the big things, and Tony Blair's big things will be peace in Northern Ireland, democracy in Iraq and the flinging out of the Taliban and al-Qaida in Afghanistan.

'. . . After 9/11 he stuck to the war on terror and had the guts to support America when America most needed it. He had the guts to stick with that support and not resile from it, even though he came under enormous political pressure to do so. I admire him for that and I think history will too.' – Historian Andrew Roberts, 10 May 2007.

'He has been steadfast in the face of negative opinion, and in the face of crises he has stood steady. We could count on him.' – Former US Secretary of State Colin Powell, 10 May 2007.

'Blair revitalised his party, modernised his country's economy and its approach to social problems and took the lead on global issues. I'm glad he was there and grateful for our friendship.' – Bill Clinton, 10 May 2007.

'When Tony Blair tells you something, as we say in Texas, you can take it to the bank.' – President George W. Bush, 10 May 2007.

'As a man of genuine faith he has not shied away from confronting extremism, while respecting difference.' – Rowan Williams, Archbishop of Canterbury, 10 May 2007.

'He could have done so much more and did not need to make the Iraq mistake. But what he did is still substantial. A good man, a great politician. He left his country in better shape than when he found it and established a new political system. He will be a tough act to follow.' – Will Hutton, *Observer*, 13 May 2007.

Against

'Unwanted and unloved, despised, dishonoured and perhaps disgraced. The modest achievements of his government at the margins are far outweighed by its failures and follies. Above all, his personal contribution has been a wrong-headed foreign policy and a disastrous war. Quite apart from the catastrophe in Iraq, what so many people have come to loathe is the tone of his regime. The whiff of corruption has become a stench. The alleged sale of peerages may be the greatest scandal this country has seen for generations . . . This is a man who has lost all contact with reality. Indeed, over the weird final phase of his career, his detachment from the real world is almost pathological.' – Geoffrey Wheatcroft, from his book *Yo, Blair!*

'Ever since the Formula One scandal Blair has thought he walked on water. Gifts, loans, gongs, coronets, jobs are to him the small change of power. He is a man who has waged five wars and rubbed shoulders with princes and presidents. Whenever charged with making a mistake he declares his accountability to his Maker and history. Mortals merit not apology but charm.

'Can Blair now salvage any dignity, if not legacy, from his endgame? His references to hospitals and schools look threadbare as the scale of waste in his turbulent reforms becomes ever more apparent. His visits to world trouble spots are desperate, as are his orotund appeals to the world to save itself from mistakes he did so little in office to correct. He has run out of time to engineer an honourable retreat from Iraq. Why he failed to remove Gordon Brown from the Treasury or why he broke his pledge to stay a full term remain a mystery. He seems in retrospect a shilly-shallying leader with no killer instinct.

'Total command over the machinery of government has been the hallmark of Blair's style, as taught by his mentor, Margaret Thatcher.' – Simon Jenkins, *Sunday Times*, 4 February 2007.

'Lies, lies and more lies. More sleaze than the Conservatives ever had and a willingness to lead us even further into the murky world of the Labour Party's "paradise".' – Linda from Cheshire, posted on the Downing Street website, 19 February 2007.

'In 1997 I thought he was the Messiah. Six years on I looked at Tony and heard Iraqi and Palestinian children crying. Some things cannot be undone.' – Lauren Booth, Cherie Blair's half-sister, *Mail on Sunday*, 22 April 2007.

'Just as he has all but destroyed the soul of the Labour Party, so Tony Blair has inflicted overwhelming damage to the structures and institutions of the British state in recent years. He has sidelined Parliament, subverted the intelligence services, compromised the judiciary and debauched the civil service. As a result, the qualities we used to be able to rely on from public figures – decency, integrity, honesty – no longer exist.' – Peter Oborne, *Daily Mail*, 28 April 2007.

'The Blair years have been a boom time for: Ann Summers sex shops (up from 13 to 134 since 1997); free Viagra; CCTV cameras; wind farms; John Prescott; Peter Mandelson; Cherie Blair's lecture income; the prison population; Alastair Campbell; private security guards; sales of illegal drugs; binge-drinking; City salaries; Ken Livingstone; childhood obesity; and grossly incompetent management of the rail system.

'The Blair era has been one long reality TV show, quite as repellent in its way as *Big Brother*.' – Max Hastings, *Daily Mail*, 28 April 2007.

'In hindsight, it turned out he was just a politician like all the rest. I was brought up a Labour voter and it was euphoric when they got into power. I didn't realise it wasn't New Labour at all – it was the Tories dressed in red.' – Noel Gallagher, 1 May 2007.

'When Labour came to power they brought with them all the black arts of sharp practice and spin that they had perfected in opposition. One of the most dismal legacies of the New Labour legacy has been to turn government into a marketing exercise. The electorate now know that they were sold a pup.

"'Twenty-four hours to save the NHS," cried Labour on 30 April 1997. 87,600 hours later, what exactly has been achieved?' – John Major, 2 May 2007.

'I feel disappointed in the way he waged war on Iraq, the double standards in UK foreign policy. The way he has been with America. He has made Britain lose credibility on the diplomatic stage. People no longer respect our country.' – Mohammad Shafiq, former supporter turned Liberal Democrat, 10 May 2007.

'He embraced market ideology with the uncritical fervour of the convert. The poor never heard that they came first.' – Polly Toynbee, *Guardian*, 10 May 2007.

'The great skills of ambiguity, broad strategy and ready compromise which made Blair so electable are not the skills needed to effect change.' – William Hague, 9 May 2007.

'This man is vainer than Narcissus and more arrogant than Napoleon.' – Ann Widdecombe, 11 May 2007.

'His judgement was often flawed and he stayed on far too long.' – Former Labour Chancellor Lord Healey, 10 May 2007.

'Tony Blair's legacy can be summed up in one word: Iraq.' – SNP leader Alex Salmond, 10 May 2007.

Undecided

'I feel like he's a man trapped. I don't think he's cold hearted, and I think he must suffer. He must do. You see those images of Iraq and Afghanistan and Lebanon, don't you? And I suspect somewhere, when he goes home at night and the kids are in bed, he must go, "Jesus, what have I done?"' – Actor Robert Lindsay, who played Blair in *A Very Social Secretary* (2005) and *The Trial of Tony Blair* (2007), February 2007.

'I first came across Tony Blair in France in 1996. We had a conversation about the election and he said he enjoyed the stuff we did about John Major. I said: "When you get into power it will be stuff about you." He said: "Yeah, and how does Lord Bremner sound?" which was funny then but it's a lot funnier now.' – Impressionist Rory Bremner, *Times*, 20 February 2007.

'I have a healthy respect for the Prime Minister's skills – healthy respect, as in the time I once met Muhammad Ali and shook the greatest fist of the twentieth century. Blair is one of the great political talents of his age, singular and mysterious in his self-possession and inner reliance.' – Henry Porter, *Observer*, 25 February 2007.

'Our constitution has now been almost completely refashioned by the Blair government, and is coming to be based on consciously formulated rules rather than tacit understanding. We have been living, therefore, through an unnoticed constitutional revolution, a quiet revolution yet profound.' – Constitutional expert Vernon Bogdanor, *House Magazine*, 5 March 2007.

The verdict

'Blair seems destined to be remembered as a consummately skilful political operator with brilliant tactical instincts but no radical or compelling long-term vision.

'When the dust settles, he is likely to be found in the middle-to-upper reaches of the prime ministerial league tables, rubbing shoulders with the likes of Baldwin and Wilson: moderate modernisers, perennial election-winners, consummate salesmen, pretty straight kind of guys.' – Dominic Sandbrook, *Observer*, 8 April 2007.

'This story of wasted opportunity will seem oddly personal. For Tony Blair was a man blessed with the rarest of talents, surely the best communicator to dominate British politics since Churchill. Even when he was counted out, he somehow bounced back.

'And yet, the first line of his obituary will record that Tony Blair made history by winning three elections – and by fighting a tragically needless war.' – Jonathan Freedland, *Guardian*, 10 May 2007.

'Tony Blair may not be missed here in London. But as the West's senior statesman, he will be missed on the international stage. He has been the leader who has best articulated an activist role for the international community in dealing with environmental catastrophe, extreme poverty in Africa, the ideological battle with al-Qaida and other Islamic extremists, and the need for moral intervention. Sadly, it is his support for George Bush's catastrophic decisions in the Iraq war that most will remember.' – James P. Rubin, US assistant Secretary of State in the Clinton administration, 10 May 2007.

Author's verdict

Saint Tony or Judas Blair? Successor to Clement Attlee or Margaret Thatcher? Family man or baby-killer?

The complexities and inconsistencies in Tony Blair's character and record in office have polarised the nation. He has presided over a massively unpopular war, a tsunami of sleaze allegations and a welter of disappointments, and has engaged in a long-running feud with his successor, Gordon Brown. But together they have also steered Britain through an unprecedented period of economic growth and increased prosperity and they have reached an astonishing peace settlement in Northern Ireland.

Blair, with his memoirs, lecture tours and new roles on the world stage, is determined to leave a lasting legacy and to be regarded as one of those few politicians who has pushed Britain in a new direction towards real, long-lasting and beneficial change. Unfortunately, such judgements are not within his remit alone, and the political and internal party wounds inflicted in recent years remain red raw.

Critics point to the ongoing conflicts in Iraq and Afghanistan, a widening gap between rich and poor, the destruction of institutions, including possibly the UK itself, creeping privatisation, and the rise of both a Big Brother state and a nanny state. Supporters point to falling unemployment, a rise in opportunities, greater investment in public services and a fairer, more tolerant nation. They might be talking about two different men, two different decades and two different countries. But Tony Blair, both of them, is guaranteed more than a footnote in the history books.

He is the first Labour leader to win three consecutive general elections and the first to serve ten years. He is also the first serving Prime Minister to be interviewed by the police in an ongoing criminal investigation. He is the first national leader for several generations to stress his Christian faith, and the first to invite known drug-users to No. 10 during his early unfortunate flirtation with 'Cool Britannia'. And that is the trouble with instant verdicts on Blair, his administration and his legacy: there are so many contradictions.

On coming to power, after years of Tory sleaze, greed and scandal, Blair promised never to be seduced by the trappings of power and later warned New Labour it had to be 'whiter than white'. Since then we have had Formula One; the love lives of the late Robin Cook, David Blunkett and John Prescott; Cheriegate; the double resignations of Peter Mandelson and Blunkett; 'a good day to get out anything we want to bury'; the dodgy dossier; the suicide of David Kelly; super-casinos and the expensive flop of the Millennium Dome; cash-for-access, cash-for-passports and the protracted cash-for-peerages, still far from over.

On the domestic front we have seen unprecedented billions of pounds extra poured into public services, paid for by rises in indirect taxation, but much of the cash has been swallowed up by mismanaged pay deals to doctors and administrators, and by unnecessary experiments involving the semi-privatisation of education.

The rich have got richer and the power of trade unions to protect the rights of their members, castrated by Margaret Thatcher, has not been restored. But unemployment is half that of the Thatcherite peak and the national minimum wage has benefited millions.

We have seen freedoms covering the age of gay sex consent, civil partnership and cannabis possession expanded but personal freedoms covering smoking and drinking diminished. We have witnessed an explosion in CCTV and other monitoring methods, efforts to prolong detention without charge and Britain's complicity in the abuse of human rights epitomised by Guantanamo Bay. But the terrorist attack on the London transport system, and other foiled attempts at mass murder, showed brutally that the threat from home-grown Islamic suicide bombers is no myth. We have seen decent immigrant families rounded up and expelled in an effort to reduce the asylum and immigration figure, yet convicted foreign criminals have escaped deportation.

Priority has been given to curbing anti-social behaviour and violent crime is down, but ASBOs are now worn as a badge of pride by many youngsters and too many communities remain blighted by crime. Regeneration cash has been targeted on run-down urban areas, giving existing property-owners a boost but leaving younger people priced out of the housing market.

Pensioners have benefited from free TV licences, free off-peak travel and increases in fuel payments, but the black hole in occupational pension schemes suggests that their grandchildren could be the first generation to be poorer than their parents.

The House of Lords and other venerable institutions have been radically overhauled but, in the words of Tony Booth, Tory toffs have been replaced by Tony's cronies.

Scotland and Wales have won devolved parliaments but, in the north at least, that could still result in the dismemberment of the UK. And Blair may have led the Labour Party to victory three times, but party membership has more than halved, Labour councillors have been decimated and party activists have drifted away.

Two genuine achievements stand out, and will continue to do so when historians publish the long view. Blair more than anyone else, through his diplomatic efforts and toughness, halted the ethnic cleansing of Kosovans. He cut through the complexities of the former Yugoslavia, built a coalition with NATO and persuaded America that the world would not countenance genocide. He was born in the post-war era and the accounts of Auschwitz and other death camps were part of his childhood. The images of internees in Slobodan Milošević's brutal grip were not ones he could ignore.

And he stuck with the Northern Ireland peace process, the initiative started by John Major to end a conflict which, when he took over, seemed insoluble and which had claimed 3,350 lives. Blair embarked on a seemingly endless series of negotiations, conferences and summits with no ideological baggage, banged heads together, cajoled, charmed and refused to give in or back down. He won, fingers crossed. It may prove to be his greatest achievement.

And now we come to Iraq.

The stubbornness Blair deployed to good effect across the Irish Sea came to the fore after the 9/11 attacks on New York and Washington. The toppling of the Afghan Taliban regime, sponsors and hosts of al-Qaida, was a natural and inevitable response. The subsequent invasion of Iraq was more problematical.

Blair, during whistle-stop global tours, initially held back American action as he tried to build a genuine anti-Saddam coalition and win a clear UN mandate. He failed, but stuck to his promises to George Bush, leading to charges that he was the President's poodle. He ignored the wishes of a million anti-war marchers in London and many more across the country.

The conventional war was quickly won, but the aftermath has been a nightmare in which 150 British servicemen and women, more than 3,000 American personnel and possibly 100,000 Iraqi insurgents and civilians have died.

Blair believed, because he wanted to, briefings on Saddam's weapons of mass destruction. He can be forgiven that. He knew they once existed because Britain, the United States, the former Soviet Union and other nations had sold them to the dictator. But he assumed that America had prepared for the recon-struction of Iraq, had in place a viable peace-keeping plan and had at least a vague exit strategy. He assumed wrongly. Nevertheless a cruel fascistic despot is in his grave and two-thirds of Iraqis braved bombings, murder and intimidation to vote in their first post-Saddam elections, a turn-out which puts Britain's recent electoral record to shame.

On Iraq, I believe the jury is still out – but that is also true of the Blair record and legacy. My instincts are that he will be judged a consummate politician but, like Churchill, Wilson and Thatcher, a flawed national leader. Given that company, he may not be too unhappy with such a verdict.